MW00636785

Punctuation for Clarity and Style

A Core Curriculum Workshop
of the American Medical Writers Association

LYNN M. ALPERIN

AMERICAN
MEDICAL WRITERS
ASSOCIATION
The Resource for Medical Communicators

KENDALL/HUNT PUBLISHING COMPANY
4050 Westmark Drive   Dubuque, Iowa 52002

ISBN 13: 978-0-7575-3381-5
ISBN 10: 0-7575-3381-7

Printed in the United States of America
10 9 8 7 6 5 4 3 2 1

Acknowledgments

Remarkable sharing of professional knowledge characterizes the American Medical Writers Association (AMWA). From this shared expertise has grown AMWA's outstanding educational program. This workshop is a byproduct of that special attribute of the association and of its cadre of talented members who collaborate so generously.

I owe a special debt of thanks to Helen Hodgson, PhD, who many years ago plucked me out of blissful anonymity and who has been responsible for many of my assignments as I rose through the ranks of AMWA. Helen was always there to assuage my doubts and to assure me that "Of course, you can do it!" Marianne Mallia, ELS, has also been a cherished cheerleader, encouraging me on to achievements that I feared were unattainable. And I would be remiss were I not to acknowledge AMWA's former executive director, Lillian Sablack, who first asked me to lead "Punctuation for Clarity and Style." Edwina Davis and Mary Knatterud, PhD, were early leaders of this course; I admire their knowledge and skill and have learned much about punctuation from them. Also, I am grateful to Edie Schwager and Norman Grossblatt, ELS (D), who serve as examples of how fine an editor really can be—both of them have been inspirations to me.

Sue Hudson managed this project magnficently; she, Helen Hodgson, and Marianne Mallia spent many hours reviewing the the first complete draft of the module and provided valuable critiques. Flo Witte, MA, ELS, provided initial guidance and scrupulously copyedited the final draft; James Cozzarin, ELS, and Stephen N. Palmer, PhD, ELS, reviewed multiple-choice questions in the final draft. I am indebted to these excellent reviewers for fine-tuning the workshop to the greatest extent possible. For any errors that remain, I claim sole responsibility.

Shortly after I started this project, AMWA offered a workshop on constructing test questions. Having never written multiple-choice questions, I signed up immediately. What I learned from Joan Lorenz at that workshop enabled me to write the many exercises you will find herein. I cannot begin to thank her for filling this void in my knowledge and for reviewing many of the exercises.

Cheryl Iverson, ELS, has kept me abreast of changes for the forthcoming 10th edition of the *American Medical Association Manual of Style*. I appreciate her taking time from her enormous task as chair of the AMA Style Manual Committee to help me add currency to this module. And as AMWA president, Dominic De Bellis, PhD, led the way and gave valued support at the outset of the project. My thanks go to all these friends and colleagues and to the many others who have helped me create this distance-learning workshop.

Contents

Introduction

The educational program of the American Medical Writers Association (AMWA) supports our mission "to promote standards of excellence in medical communication." Accordingly, our workshops are designed to do just that—to raise our writing and editing skills to a higher level in our ongoing quest for excellence. The AMWA Core Curriculum focuses on the skills and competencies that we need to develop professional expertise. For some of us, Core Curriculum workshops provide helpful review; for others, the basic tools of our trade. Over the past 20 years, the AMWA workshop program has grown tremendously in response to increasing demand for continuing education.

To meet this demand and to reach a broader segment of our membership, AMWA has embarked on a series of distance-learning workshops. The first self-study module, *Basic Grammar and Usage*, was introduced in 2003. The subject of punctuation is the logical next step to build upon a firm grammatical foundation. As with the first module in this series, *Punctuation for Clarity and Style* enables medical writers and editors to hone their skills without incurring the expense of traveling to conferences.

Why all this emphasis on a handful or two of innocent little marks? Are they really so important that we must master the many rules that govern their use? By the time you have completed this module, I hope to have convinced you that these seemingly innocuous marks can pack a powerful punch.

In the course of leading this workshop at AMWA annual and chapter conferences, I have learned that many medical writers and editors feel quite uncomfortable with punctuation. They either never learned the rules in the first place, have forgotten them, or (scariest of all) don't care one way or the other, relying solely on their intuition for guidance. Whether you are learning new skills or sharpening old skills, this module is intended to arm you with logical ways to think about punctuation and with the most useful rules to help you in your work. The workshop is designed to approach these rules as pragmatically as possible, with many medical examples. We will look at the rules together and try to understand why indicated exceptions make sense.

As the title of the workshop states, we are concerned with clarity. Quintilian, a Roman rhetorician who lived in the first century AD, set the standard for clarity: "clear writing is writing that is incapable of being misunderstood" (Zeiger, p 2). Clear, precise writing is essential to medical communication. Proper sentence structure certainly contributes to clearly written material, but punctuation is often the final touch that ensures clarity. My favorite description of punctuation comes from *The Gregg Reference Manual* (Sabin, p 4):

> Punctuation marks are the mechanical means for making the meaning of a sentence easily understood. They indicate the proper relationships between words, phrases, and clauses when word order alone is not sufficient to make these relationships clear.

So while clarity is our undisputed goal, the logic of relationships underlies our efforts to achieve this goal. And punctuation quietly enables us to express and emphasize those relationships— quietly, because "the best punctuation is that which the reader is unaware of" (Skillen, p 172).

Punctuation helps medical writers achieve the precision and accuracy that are so crucial in science. Descriptions must be clear enough to enable readers to validate results by replicating them. We are writing for busy readers, so succinctness is also a virtue. Ambiguity is not acceptable, and scientific writing tends more toward formality than informality. This, then, is the framework within which we apply the rules of punctuation.

Style is the other goal of this workshop. What do we mean by "style?" *Merriam-Webster's Collegiate Dictionary* provides a number of definitions for this word, two of which are relevant to the study of punctuation: "a distinctive manner of expression" and "a convention with respect to spelling, punctuation, capitalization, and typographic arrangement and display followed in writing or printing."

For our purposes, style encompasses both of these definitions. Style includes using the full range of punctuation marks at our disposal to make our writing more interesting, more varied, more emphatic, and more lively, as well as using the conventions that are unique to medicine. Teaching this workshop, I have learned sadly that a great many medical writers and editors do not use—indeed, do not even own—a style manual. Style manuals are essential tools of our trade, and our knowledge of their rules and conventions contributes greatly to our professional expertise. Being able to cite rules from respected style manuals enhances our credibility and authority.

Many style manuals are available, although some companies choose to develop their own "house" styles. No one style is necessarily better than another, but we should know which styles are accepted for the work we are doing and follow those styles consistently. For medical writers and editors, the most commonly used style manuals are the *American Medical Association Manual of Style* (AMA) and *Scientific Style and Format: The CBE Manual for Authors, Editors, and Publishers* (CBE [note that in 2000, the Council of Biology Editors was renamed the Council of Science Editors]). Although these two style manuals agree on many points, they differ on some. In general, clinical writing tends to follow AMA style, whereas the CBE style manual contains certain conventions that may be more useful for the basic sciences and some that pertain to international practices in scientific writing. This module will adhere primarily to AMA style as it is used in American English; some points on which AMA and CBE differ will be noted.

I encourage you to identify the style manuals most appropriate for your work and to make them well-worn fixtures on your desktop. A general style manual, such as *The Chicago Manual of Style* or *The Gregg Reference Manual*, is helpful as a backup to answer questions that may not be covered in the scientific manuals. Applying the rules with consistency is an additional step you can take to make your writing clearer for your reader.

Overall, the objectives of this workshop are to enhance the following skills:

- ◆ Recognition of common grammatical constructions involving punctuation
- ◆ Use of editing techniques to eliminate awkward or excessive punctuation
- ◆ Ability to vary punctuation to enhance clarity, emphasis, and liveliness
- ◆ Familiarity with medical style conventions

Before you jump in with both feet, you should know a few things about this workshop. The module is organized into chapters that cover the major punctuation marks and some of the medical style conventions. At the end of each chapter, you will find exercises with which you can test yourself to see how well you have learned the material in that chapter. I suggest that you do not progress to the next chapter until you feel you have a good grasp of what has been presented thus far. Please resist the temptation to skip around; instead, take up each chapter in the order in which it appears, because each new chapter will assume your knowledge of material that has been covered earlier.

Answers to the chapter exercises may be found at the back of the module, along with a glossary, a bibliography, an index, and a final examination. Definitions of terms that appear in boldface throughout the module are provided in the Glossary. In many examples, certain punctuation marks have been bolded or changed from italics for added emphasis. The Bibliography lists a number of excellent reference books, some of which are cited parenthetically in the text. All page numbers cited from the *American Medical Association Manual of Style* refer only to the 9th edition; changes planned for the 10th edition, slated for publication in 2007, are cited as "written communication."

So much for the preamble. As you work through the module, enjoy the process of sharpening your skills. To apply for Core Curriculum credit, please complete the final examination and send it to AMWA in accordance with the accompanying directions. I hope that when you have completed this workshop, you will have gained greater confidence in your use of punctuation and be better prepared to defend and support your punctuation decisions.

Essential Concepts

that that is is that that is not is not is that not so

When I (as a participant) ventured into this workshop many years ago, the AMWA workshop leader, Edwina Davis, had just finished writing the 14 words above on a blackboard. I think it is fair to say that although we know what each of these words means, at first—and even second, third, and fourth—glance, they do not make any sense at all. See if you can make them into a coherent statement, retaining their current arrangement. I have never forgotten these words because they illustrate so effectively the essential role punctuation plays in written communication.

Being able to transmit complex, technical information through the use of 26 little letters (the basic units, or "atoms," of the English language) is amazing when we think about it. These letters have help, however, as they form words, phrases, clauses, sentences, and paragraphs. But until punctuation is introduced, these elements may make as little sense as the 14 seemingly unrelated words above. Punctuation marks will provide the crucial missing link needed to define the relationships among these grammatical elements.

REVIEW OF SENTENCE ANATOMY

Before we can apply the rules governing punctuation, we must understand the elements of grammar onto which punctuation is superimposed. The following review should ensure that the terms used in the module hold the same meaning for all of us.

Subjects and predicates

A **sentence** is a group of words containing a **subject** and a **predicate** and expressing a complete thought. What exactly do the terms "subject" and "predicate" mean?

> **Subject = any sort of entity.** A subject may be a person, place, object, concept, pronoun that refers to something identified elsewhere, or action functioning as a noun.
>
> *The surgeon completed the operation.*
>
> **Predicate = some information about the subject.** The predicate may either describe the subject or identify an action that the subject performs or that is performed upon it.
>
> *The surgeon completed the lengthy operation.*

The predicate (underlined in the preceding example) contains the **transitive verb** *completed* and its **direct object,** *operation.* A transitive verb requires a direct object to complete its meaning; the direct object is the person or thing that receives the action of the **verb** or upon which the verb's action is performed. Note that the predicate includes the verb <u>and</u> the verb's object plus any of their modifiers, in this case the adjective *lengthy.*

A transitive verb may also take an **indirect object,** which is the person or thing on whose behalf, to whom, or for whom the action of the verb is performed.

> The nurse handed <u>the surgeon</u> a scalpel.

In this sentence, the direct object *a scalpel* is handed <u>*to*</u> the surgeon, making *the surgeon* the indirect object.

Now, compare the predicates in the following sentences:

> The surgeon <u>completed the lengthy operation.</u> *what*

> The surgeon <u>collapsed after the lengthy procedure.</u> *when*

Again, the predicates are underlined. How do the predicates differ from each other in these two sentences? The first sentence above contains a transitive verb that required a direct object telling what was completed. In the second sentence, the predicate *collapsed after the lengthy procedure* consists of the **intransitive verb** *collapsed* as well as its adverbial modifier (the prepositional phrase *after the lengthy procedure*), which indicates when the action of the verb occurred. The verb *collapsed* is intransitive because it does not need a direct object to complete its meaning.

The next example contains a third kind of verb, called a **linking verb.** Linking verbs are usually forms of the verb *to be* or of verbs of the senses (eg, *feel, look,* and *smell*). A linking verb does not take a direct object or an indirect object but does need some additional information to complete its meaning. This additional information is called a **complement** because it completes a linking verb. (Direct and indirect objects are also considered complements because they, too, complete the verbs they follow.) Examples of linking verbs and complements follow.

> The surgeon <u>was exhausted.</u>
> [The verb *is was*; the complement *is exhausted*]

> The patient <u>felt unable to empathize.</u>
> [The verb is *felt*; the complement, *unable to empathize.*]

Some sentences contain two or more subjects (<u>*Smoking and drinking* may damage your health</u>) or predicates (*The patient <u>smoked cigarettes and drank herself to death</u>*); these are called **compound subjects** and **compound predicates,** respectively.

Now we'll turn to other sentence elements that may be found in either the subject or the predicate. Understanding what these elements are and being able to identify them will help us apply punctuation rules.

Clauses vs phrases

Clauses and phrases are the main subgroups found within a sentence. A **clause** contains both a subject and a predicate. The two types of clauses are independent and dependent. Their characteristics are shown in the box below:

Clause = subject + predicate

Independent (main):   can stand alone as a complete sentence
Dependent (subordinate): cannot stand alone

An **independent clause** can be a complete sentence. When an independent clause is in a sentence that also contains a dependent clause, the independent clause may be referred to as the main clause. The following sentence is an independent clause:

Hemoglobin electrophoresis detected an abnormality.

A **dependent clause** depends on the rest of the sentence to complete its meaning. A dependent clause must be attached to an independent clause and is often introduced by a **subordinating conjunction** (eg, *however, although, while, because, if,* or *since*) or by a **relative pronoun** (eg, *who, whom, whose, which,* or *that*). The independent clause shown above can be turned into a dependent clause, which must then be attached to an independent clause to become a complete thought (a sentence).

Example: *Although hemoglobin electrophoresis detected an abnormality,* the patient reported no symptoms.

In this example, the dependent (or subordinate) clause beginning with the subordinating conjunction *although* is separated from but attached to the independent clause, *the patient reported no symptoms.* The rules for punctuating clauses will be presented in the chapters that follow on commas, semicolons, and colons.

Phrase = related words missing either a subject or a verb

A phrase is not expected to stand alone.

Lacking either a subject or a verb, a **phrase** is less substantial than a clause. Phrases serve usually as modifiers of nouns and verbs. The two kinds of modifying phrases are the **prepositional phrase** and the **participial phrase**:

◆ **Prepositional**
   during the day
   after work
   before the operation

◆ **Participial**

> *Running through the halls,* Dr. Smith collided with an orderly. – *Noun*
> *Purchased in 2000,* this instrument is already obsolete. – *adjective*

The participial phrase *Running through the halls* becomes a **gerund** phrase, however, if used as a noun: eg, in the sentence *Running through the halls is prohibited,* this phrase is the subject. Participial phrases function as adjectives, whereas gerund phrases serve as nouns.

To punctuate properly requires being able to distinguish clauses from phrases. (The **infinitive** phrase *To punctuate properly* serves as the subject in the preceding sentence.)

Restrictive vs nonrestrictive elements

Accurate scientific writing requires a clear distinction between restrictive and nonrestrictive material. Information that is needed to complete the meaning of a sentence is called a **restrictive (essential) element**; in contrast, possibly interesting but unnecessary information is called a **nonrestrictive (nonessential) element**. Restrictive and nonrestrictive elements may be words, phrases, or clauses. Examples of sentences containing restrictive and nonrestrictive elements follow.

> **Restrictive:** *Patients who met the qualifications were placed on the protocol.*

The underlined clause, *who met the qualifications,* restricts the meaning of the sentence to a group that is presumably smaller than the larger group of patients who may have been considered initially for the protocol. If the clause were omitted, the sentence would read *Patients were placed on the protocol,* and the information telling the reader "which patients" would have been lost. Therefore, in this sentence, the clause is necessary.

> **Nonrestrictive:** *Patients with hemophilia, who bleed easily, may be given factor VIII.*

The clause *who bleed easily* does not restrict the meaning of this sentence. By definition, patients with hemophilia bleed easily, so while this clause may add interesting information to a reader who does not know this, the meaning of the sentence would not be changed by the clause's omission.

The challenge with these elements is that sometimes a clause may be either restrictive or nonrestrictive, depending on the context; understanding the context becomes crucial to achieving proper punctuation. Examples are provided in the following discussion of relative clauses. But first, let's look at appositives, phrases, and clauses, all forms in which restrictive and nonrestrictive elements often appear.

Appositives

An **appositive** is "a noun or noun phrase that identifies another noun or pronoun that immediately precedes it" (Sabin, p. 636):

> *The president of the university, Dr. Baldwin, will expect you at the meeting.*

In the sentence above, *Dr. Baldwin* is a nonrestrictive appositive. We can assume that the university has only one president, so learning his name in this sentence may be interesting or helpful but is not essential to the sense of the sentence. In contrast, look at the next example:

> *The species Homo sapiens is distinguished from other species by . . . .*

If this <u>restrictive appositive</u>, which identifies the species being discussed, were omitted, the sentence would be unclear because the reader would not know which species was being distinguished from the other species.

Phrases

Phrases, which do not contain both a subject and a predicate, may also be restrictive or nonrestrictive. How would you determine whether the underlined phrase in the following sentences is restrictive or nonrestrictive?

The application <u>requesting the funds for equipment</u> was denied.

If the phrase *requesting the funds for equipment* were removed, the reader would not be able to distinguish this application from applications requesting funds for other purposes, so the phrase is treated here as a restrictive element. But suppose only one application had been submitted. If that were the case, then a sentence treating the phrase as nonrestrictive would be appropriate:

The application, <u>requesting the funds for equipment</u>, was denied.

Clauses

Dependent clauses may be restrictive or nonrestrictive as well, depending on the context in which they are placed. One type of dependent clause that we often encounter is introduced by a relative pronoun (*who, whom, which,* or *that*) and is called a **relative clause**. Determining whether these clauses are restrictive or not carries a two-pronged responsibility for writers: both the use or absence of punctuation and the choice (when the choices are *that* or *which*) of which relative pronoun is appropriate must be decided. The rules for relative clauses and examples of their application will be discussed in Chapter 2, so only a couple of examples will be shown here:

Restrictive: *Articles <u>that have been published</u> will no longer be considered.*

Nonrestrictive: *Downsizing the laboratory staff, <u>which grew while the research was being conducted</u>, is our current priority.*

The basic rule is straightforward: restrictive clauses are introduced by *that* and are <u>not</u> set off by commas; nonrestrictive clauses are introduced by *which* and <u>are</u> set off by commas.

Types of sentences

Sentences are defined in terms of the number and types of clauses they contain. To apply the rules of punctuation, we must be able to recognize the different types of sentences. All sentences fall into one of the following four categories. See if you can identify the independent clauses and the dependent clauses in the examples below:

A **simple sentence** consists of one independent clause.

Results of the radiographs and of the laboratory studies indicated adenocarcinoma.

A **compound sentence** consists of two or more independent clauses.

The doctor saw the patient and left; the nurse began to prepare the patient for discharge.

A **complex sentence** consists of one independent clause and at least one dependent clause.

Although the test results were not yet available, the physician already suspected the patient's diagnosis.

A **compound-complex sentence** consists of at least two independent clauses and one or more dependent clauses.

When the technician had completed the transfusion, the patient was returned to the medicine unit, and the doctor hurried to the lecture hall.

Now that we have reviewed the necessary terminology, we can begin to talk seriously about punctuation.

PUNCTUATION POWER

We have already learned that punctuation marks are used to define relationships among the elements within a sentence. Learning which marks to use when will be the primary task for the rest of this workshop. Some marks insert breaks between elements; other marks connect related elements. Knowing the relative strength of the various breaks helps us know which marks to use. The box that follows shows these marks, starting with the strongest break and ending with the weakest.

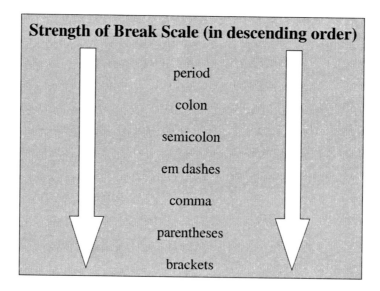

Strength of Break Scale (in descending order)

period

colon

semicolon

em dashes

comma

parentheses

brackets

Each of these punctuation marks has a different strength and serves a unique function. Once we have learned these marks, we can use them to emphasize different points in our writing. Let's "play" with the following three pieces of information just to see how punctuation can shift the emphasis of different elements and perhaps alter the interpretation of the sentences.

The doctor has a problem. He administered the wrong drug. The patient died.
Three separate ideas are expressed here. Each simple sentence ends with a period. Whether any relationship exists among the three events is unknown.

The doctor has a problem: he administered the wrong drug and the patient died.
The **colon** used here sets the reader up to view the administration of the wrong drug and the patient's death as the doctor's problems. Perhaps the doctor needs a lawyer?

The doctor has a problem; he administered the wrong drug. The patient died.
With the use of the semicolon, the relationship between the doctor's problem and the administration of the wrong drug is implied but not as forcefully as it was with the colon. The strong break setting off the patient's death seems to remove it from the problem.

The doctor has a problem—he administered the wrong drug and the patient died.
Although less strongly than the colon, the **em dash** here tends to emphasize the action and the outcome by visually calling attention to what happened.

The doctor, who administered the wrong drug, has a problem; and the patient died.
Changing the drug error into a nonrestrictive relative clause changes the meaning of the sentence. The doctor's problem could be anything. The patient's death after the semicolon almost seems to be an afterthought.

The following sentences, with the same structure but different punctuation, show other ways of emphasizing or de-emphasizing specific pieces of information in the sentence:

The doctor (who administered the wrong drug) has a problem, and the patient died.
The doctor who administered the wrong drug has a problem (and the patient died).
The doctor who administered the wrong drug has a problem, and the patient died!

These variations are perhaps silly, but they should demonstrate the importance of selecting the best punctuation marks for conveying a given message.

APPROACHES TO EFFECTIVE PUNCTUATION

Various approaches may be taken to punctuation, and some changes have occurred with the passage of time. Three different issues are worthy of brief discussion here.

Open vs close punctuation

The question of whether to use open or close (rhymes with "gross") punctuation has been largely resolved for our purposes. **Close punctuation** is the tendency to use "as many marks as the grammatical construction will justify" (Skillin, p. 184). This approach to punctuation was common in the elaborate structure of writing in the past, sometimes resulting in text that today seems choppy and difficult to read. Consider this passage from an 1846 article in *The New Orleans Medical and Surgical Journal:*

> Thompson says, speaking of ulcers, that out of twenty surgeons, not more than one can be found who can treat ill-conditioned sores or ulcers, the consequence of wounds necessarily inflicted by themselves, in their operations. Can this be attributed to prejudice and disgust for such loathsome affections; or does it arise from the adverse and complicated distinctions of nosologists; the discrepancy of remedial agents; or, more probably, from the want of a correct knowledge of their pathology? As I have encountered the usual difficulties and have been much disappointed, in the treatment of such cases, by the routine practice of ointments, lotions, bandages, &c.; and as I have, on the other hand, been very successful in effecting cures, in some remarkable instances, by the application of a certain compound powder, I take great pleasure in now laying before the profession the result of my experience, and the means I have employed.

We no longer write like this, and as sentence structure has changed, so has punctuation. **Open punctuation** uses only as much punctuation as is required by rules of grammar or is absolutely necessary for clarity. Today, most writers and editors strive for smoother sentence structure that allows for less punctuation. Compare the differences between open and close punctuation shown in the following versions of the same sentence (Skillen, p. 184).

> **Too closely punctuated:** The soil, which, in places, overlies the hard rock of this plateau, is, for the most part, thin and poor.

> **Better:** The soil, which in places overlies the hard rock of this plateau, is for the most part thin and poor.

The first sentence is choppy and the subject, verb, and complement are almost lost among all the modifiers and commas. The second sentence, with one relative clause set off by a pair of commas, flows more smoothly and is much easier for a reader to comprehend quickly.

The trend today clearly favors open punctuation; however, Edward J. Huth, MD, suggests that a fully open style may not suit the requirements of scientific writing, and he suggests a more tempered approach (p. 60):

> When in doubt, use a mark; it will probably reduce ambiguity of meaning. . . . When meaning is clear . . . , omit punctuation that might otherwise be needed.

Scientific Style and Format (cited as CBE, p. 39) echoes this commonsense approach, embracing open punctuation but still leaning more heavily toward achieving clarity:

> When the need for a mark (or for omitting it) is not clear, the mark should be used if it will reduce or eliminate possible ambiguity.

So with some qualifications we strive for open punctuation. How do we reduce the number of punctuation marks in a sentence? Fortunately, we have editorial techniques that can help us achieve more open punctuation.

Techniques for Opening Punctuation

◆ Change word order
◆ Shorten sentence by reducing wordiness
◆ Restructure sentence
◆ Break one sentence into two or more

These techniques are used routinely in the process of editing. Let's look now at some examples to see how these techniques can be applied to reduce punctuation.

Change word order

For much of the time, Dr. Delaney, who sees 60 or more patients daily at particularly busy times, is virtually unaware of whom she is treating. (3 commas)

Dr. Delaney, who sees 60 or more patients daily at particularly busy times, is much of the time virtually unaware of whom she is treating. (2 commas)

Shorten sentence (in this case by changing adverbial phrases to adverbs) and change word order

Dr. Delaney, who sometimes sees 60 or more patients daily, is often unaware of whom she is treating. (2 commas)

The sentence above has been shortened by changing the phrase *much of the time* to the adverb *often* (which modifies the verb phrase *is unaware*) and by replacing the phrase *at particularly busy times* (which modifies the verb *sees*) with the adverb *sometimes*.

Shorten and restructure sentence

Often Dr. Delaney hardly knows whom she is treating because she sometimes sees 60 or more patients daily. (no commas)

In the sentence above, the original nonrestrictive relative clause who *sometimes sees 60 or more patients daily* has been replaced by the restrictive clause *because she sometimes sees 60 or more patients daily*, which modifies the verb *knows*. The sentence below has been broken into two simple declarative statements.

Dr. Delaney sometimes sees 60 patients daily; consequently, she is often virtually unaware of whom she is treating. (1 semicolon, 1 comma)

Be aware that parallel structure contributes greatly to clarity. Sometimes adding, modifying, or deleting one or more words can reinforce parallelism in the sentence structure, thereby removing ambiguity—as well as the need for a punctuation mark.

Confusing: *The company has begun incorporating the technological advances and production of the new device.*

Clearer: *The company has begun incorporating the technological advances and producing the new drug.*

Break one sentence into two or more—but only when appropriate.

I would not recommend splitting the sentence about Dr. Delaney into two sentences. Doing so would separate cause (being too busy and seeing too many patients) and effect (hardly knowing whom she is treating) unnecessarily. However, some sentences that are less cohesive do need to be separated.

Adaptable vs rigid punctuation

The issue of whether to take an adaptable or a rigid approach to punctuation was spelled out beautifully by H. L. Mencken (pp. 196–197):

> With precious few exceptions, all the books on style in English are by writers quite unable to write. The subject, indeed, seems to exercise a special and dreadful fascination over school ma'm [*sic*], bucolic college professors, and other such pseudoliterates. . . . Their central aim, of course, is to reduce the whole thing to a series of simple rules—the overmastering passion of their melancholy order, at all times and everywhere.

Although Mencken's position may be a little extreme, this quotation raises the important question "How flexible should we be in applying the rules of punctuation?" The need for accuracy in scientific writing makes a strong adherence to the rules an obligation for those of us in biomedical communication; however, we do not need to follow the rules so rigidly that we cannot make exceptions when they are warranted for the sake of clarity. Some rules are more compelling than others; knowing which rules must be followed and which rules can be left to an author's or editor's judgment comes with experience. In this workshop, we shall consider the hard-and-fast rules as well those that carry less obligation. The best rule of thumb is the following: make exceptions as needed to avoid ambiguity and to enhance clarity.

Routine vs creative punctuation

Variety's the very spice of life.

This quotation from William Cowper states concisely the case for creative punctuation (Cowper, p. 364a). Using a variety of marks enables us to enliven our prose, to add emphasis, and to make the written product more interesting for the reader. Although scientific writing carries with it some sense of restraint, we should be comfortable enough with the rules to use the full range of marks when appropriate.

FOUR UNDERLYING PRINCIPLES

Remember that punctuation defines <u>relationships</u> among groups of words. Developing the habit of analyzing the elements reviewed in this chapter is the first step in applying the rules of punctuation. You will find that a difficult-to-punctuate sentence is often a clue that the relationships of the elements within the sentence are impaired. When confronted with such a sentence, try to diagnose the problem, repair the sentence structure, and then insert the appropriate punctuation.

Perhaps by now you may have worked out reasonable relationships among the 14 words that appeared at the beginning of this chapter:

that that is is that that is not is not is that not so

If not, let me end your suffering. Here is a solution:

That that is, is. That that is not, is not. Is that not so?

Mary Knatterud, an outstanding AMWA workshop leader and a true punctuation maven, describes the Four "C"s of Punctuation (pp. 28–29). They offer succinct and sound advice and are the perfect note on which to conclude this preliminary chapter as we prepare to consider each punctuation mark individually.

Four "C"s of Punctuation

- ◆ **Clarity**—don't leave the flow or meaning open to doubt; don't make the reader backtrack
- ◆ **Connectedness**—don't separate unduly what logically belongs together; don't forget the second mark of a pair (of commas, quotation marks, parentheses, or brackets)
- ◆ **Conciseness**—don't clutter with excessive marks or stilted interruptions; break up long sentences
- ◆ **Consistency**—don't apply punctuation rules or options haphazardly or selectively

---

Keeping in mind that clarity is always our uppermost goal, we shall next turn our attention to our first mark—the pesky comma. But first, answer the questions in the Exercises that follow to reinforce what you have learned in this chapter.

Choose the <u>best</u> answer for each of the questions below.

1. Adverse events <u>reported by the patients</u> or <u>observed by the investigator</u> were characterized by their intensity, the action taken, and the outcome.

What are the underlined elements in this sentence?

   a. participial phrases.
   b. dependent clauses.
   c. prepositional phrases.
   d. the compound predicate.

2. While the patient was hospitalized for hypotension, she was treated also for a kidney infection; she was released after 2 weeks.

What type of sentence is the sentence above?

   a. simple.
   b. complex.
   c. compound.
   d. compound-complex.

3. Problems commonly experienced by patients taking Drug X who have participated in previous research studies <u>include</u> <u>upset stomach, tiredness, jittery or nervous feelings, difficulty sleeping, dry mouth, sweating, tremors, dizziness, or loss of appetite and weight</u>.

What is the underlined portion of this sentence?

   a. a dependent clause.
   b. the direct object of the verb.
   c. the predicate of the sentence.
   d. the indirect object of the verb.

4. In which of the following does punctuation show the proper relationships among the elements?

   a. Ultra Strength Bengay provides soothing relief from minor arthritis pain, sore aching and strained muscles, and backache.
   b. Ultra Strength Bengay provides soothing relief from minor arthritis pain, sore, aching and strained muscles, and backache.
   c. Ultra Strength Bengay provides soothing relief from minor arthritis pain; sore, aching and strained muscles, and backache.
   d. Ultra Strength Bengay provides soothing relief from minor arthritis pain; sore, aching, and strained muscles; and backache.

5. Several endoscopes <u>that can range in thickness from 2.6 mm to 4.0 mm and offer a variety of angles (30 degrees, 70 degrees, and 120 degrees)</u> are available.

What is the underlined element in this sentence?

a. a compound predicate.
b. a restrictive relative clause.
c. a nonrestrictive relative clause.
d. a restrictive phrase modifying the subject.

6. <u>Although most affected children recover completely,</u> a few reports have described development of acute leukemia in children with Down syndrome years after previous resolution of abnormal clinical and laboratory findings with TMD.

What is the underlined element in this sentence?

a. a participial phrase.
b. a dependent clause.
c. an independent clause.
d. an introductory prepositional phrase.

7. Biotechnology products will become more widely available, and, as with any new health care technology, evidence of their cost-effectiveness will be necessary.

What are the verbs in this sentence?

a. linking.
b. transitive.
c. participial.
d. intransitive.

8. In patients with horizontal mandibular excess, the alar width is often normal; in contrast, if a patient has horizontal maxillary deficiency, the alar width is frequently constricted.

Which is the dependent clause in this sentence?

a. the alar width is often normal.
b. the alar width is frequently constricted.
c. In patients with horizontal mandibular excess.
d. if a patient has horizontal maxillary deficiency.

9. The vision of the Institute is "<u>to become a center of excellence in the areas of health economics, health outcomes, and health policy research.</u>"

What is the underlined portion of this sentence?

a. the predicate.
b. the complement.
c. the direct object.
d. the indirect object.

10. <u>Assessing the function of circulating neutrophils</u> instead of neutrophils that infiltrate the lungs has two advantages: the samples are easier to collect and, more importantly, the potential local effect of *M haemolytica* on neutrophil function in situ in the lungs is removed as a confounding factor, although systemic effects of *M haemolytica* are not removed.

What is the underlined portion of this sentence?

a. the subject.
b. the predicate.
c. a participial clause.
d. an introductory clause.

The Comma (,)

2

The lowly **comma** is the most frequently used—and abused—mark in the punctuation arsenal. The comma appears in writing more often than all the other marks combined. By clarifying grammatical structure, the comma serves the critical function of saving our readers from having to sort through possible ambiguities.

How should we approach comma usage? The good news is that definite and easy-to-apply rules exist that specify when commas should, and should not, be used. The rules governing *mandatory* commas are quite clear; however, applying these rules correctly involves a strong grasp of the distinctions between phrases and clauses and between restrictive and nonrestrictive material (discussed in Chapter 1 of this study module). If you have difficulty applying the rules for commas, you may want to go back and review these distinctions. Now we will look at the rules that should enable you to use commas with greater accuracy and confidence.

The bad news (you knew there would be some, right?) is that not every situation we encounter will be covered by these lovely rules: some comma usage is subjective, and this is what can sometimes make comma usage so difficult. When confronted with the quandary of whether or not to insert an *optional* comma, we need to exercise our best judgment. You may recall the discussion of open vs close punctuation in Chapter 1; the trend toward open punctuation pertains particularly to the use of commas. Fortunately, we have guidelines to help us make the required judgments. Consider these pearls of wisdom from several authorities:

> Some writers and editors use the comma frequently to indicate what they see as a natural pause in the flow of words, but commas can be overused. The trend is to use them sparingly. A safe rule of thumb is to follow the accepted rules and use commas only when breaks are needed for sense or readability and to avoid confusion or misinterpretation (Iverson, p. 201).

> A comma should be used only if it makes the meaning clearer or enables the reader to grasp the relation of parts more quickly. Intruded commas are worse than omitted ones, but keep in mind at all times that the primary purpose of the comma is to prevent misreading (Skillin, p. 184).

For those of us writing and editing scientific material, Dr. Huth's advice that clarity is the overriding consideration in deciding whether to use an optional comma is supported by the Council of Biology Editors:

> When in doubt, use a mark; it will probably reduce ambiguity of meaning. . . . When meaning is clear . . . , omit punctuation that might otherwise be needed (Huth, p. 60).

> The present tendency is to avoid unnecessary punctuation; however, in scientific writing it is better to over-punctuate than to risk misinterpretation (CBE, p. 125).

Thus, accepting that the trend today is toward open, or less, punctuation, we must remember that open punctuation does not always best serve the cause of ensuring clarity of the subject matter with which we deal. As we learned in Chapter 1, the process of eliminating unnecessary commas may require slight rephrasing and rearrangement of words in a sentence.

Beyond unnecessary commas lie just plain incorrect commas. Consider the confusion caused by the comma in the title of Lynn Truss's delightful best-seller *Eats, Shoots & Leaves.* The explanation for the title relates that a panda enters a café, orders a sandwich, eats it, and then draws a gun and fires a couple of shots into the air. The confused waiter asks, "Why?" The panda tosses a poorly punctuated wildlife manual over his shoulder as he heads toward the door, exclaiming, "I'm a panda. Look it up." The relevant entry in the manual reads as follows: "**Panda.** Large black-and-white bear-like mammal, native to China. Eats, shoots and leaves" (Truss, jacket cover). The rule that has been ignored here warns not to use a comma to separate a verb from its object(s). Although the story of the panda is funny, the potential confusion caused by an inappropriate comma in medical information could be anything but humorous.

According to AMA style (Iverson, p. 201), "Commas, semicolons, and colons can be used to indicate a break or pause in thought, to set off material, or to introduce a new but connected thought. Each has specific uses, and the strength of the break in thought determines which mark is appropriate." Commas are the least forceful of these three marks. Let's turn now to the rules that will enable us to use commas consistently and correctly.

Use a comma

To separate
- Two independent clauses joined by a coordinating conjunction
- Items in a series or in a series of independent clauses
- Opening or ending clauses and phrases
- Contrasting expressions

To set off
- Interrupting elements
- Transitional expressions and independent comments

To indicate omission or to clarify
- Elliptical constructions
- Unusual word order

As shown in the preceding box, the functions of the comma can be grouped broadly into three categories: separating, setting off, and indicating omission or clarifying unusual word order. We will review and practice the rules for the main functions of the comma as well as the rules that dictate when *not* to use this punctuation mark.

USING COMMAS TO SEPARATE

Let's examine first the rules for the separation functions: the comma is used to separate phrases, clauses, and groups of words and to clarify the grammatical structure and the intended meaning of a sentence.

Two independent clauses joined by a coordinating conjunction

RULE: Use a comma to separate two independent clauses joined by a coordinating conjunction.

Remember that a sentence consisting of two or more independent clauses is called a compound sentence. (The mnemonic "FANBOYS" can help us remember the **coordinating conjunctions:** *for, and, nor, but, or, yet,* and *so.*) A comma should be used before the conjunction. The following sentence shows the comma preceding the coordinating conjunction *and* in accordance with the rule:

> *Fewer Hispanics than whites work in smoke-free environments, and younger workers are less protected than are older workers.*

If the independent clauses are short and the absence of a comma would not cause ambiguity, the comma may be omitted. For example, the following sentence is clear without a comma:

> *The procedure was brief and the patient recovered quickly.*

Take care not to confuse a coordinating conjunction used to link a compound predicate with the coordinating conjunction used between independent clauses. Consider the following example:

> *Since the first reported case of infection in 1890, the organism has been increasingly associated with bacteremia and currently accounts for 15% of all cases of gram-negative bacteremia.*

In this sentence, the word *and* links the compound predicate verbs *has been associated* and *accounts.* Because the phrase *currently accounts for 15% of all cases of gram-negative bacteremia* is the second predicate for the subject *the organism* and does not contain a different subject of its own, the conjunction is not separating two independent clauses. Remember that a clause must contain both a subject *and* a predicate. The second predicate is a phrase and does not qualify as an independent clause—in fact, this phrase is not any kind of clause at all—so the conjunction here cannot serve a coordinating function because the sentence has only one independent clause. In the example, a comma preceding the conjunction would erroneously separate the second verb phrase from its subject. We will discuss this construction again at the end of this chapter under the heading "When *Not* to Use a Comma."

Separating two independent clauses joined by a coordinating conjunction is a crucial function of the comma, so a bit of practice applying this rule might be helpful. Analyze the following sentences and decide whether they are punctuated properly according to this rule. If you think they are incorrect, identify the problem and correct their punctuation.

> *Interferon protects solid tissues during viral infection, interferon is also disseminated through the bloodstream during viremia, thereby protecting distant organs against the spreading infection.*

The sentence above is not correctly punctuated. Could you identify the reason why? The sentence begins with the independent clause *Interferon protects solid tissues during viral infection.* So far, so good. A second independent clause, *interferon is also disseminated through the bloodstream during viremia,* follows immediately. But a comma should not be used to separate two independent clauses <u>unless they are joined by a conjunction</u>. To correct the punctuation in this sentence, we must add an appropriate coordinating conjunction after the comma:

> *Interferon protects solid tissues during viral infection, and interferon is also disseminated through the bloodstream during viremia, thereby protecting distant organs against the spreading infection.*

An even better option here would be to replace the comma between the two clauses with a **semicolon,** as we will learn in the next chapter:

> *Interferon protects solid tissues during viral infection; interferon is also disseminated through the bloodstream during viremia, thereby protecting distant organs against the spreading infection.*

Be sure you understand that to punctuate this sentence correctly we must recognize that a comma should not separate two independent clauses that are <u>not</u> joined by a coordinating conjunction.

Consider the next sentence:

> *The upper limb parallels the clavicle and the lower limb parallels the fourth interspace.*

This sentence might slide by as is, but a comma after *clavicle,* separating the two independent clauses, will keep the reader from reading *The upper limb parallels the clavicle and the lower limb* and then having to double back to establish that *the lower limb* is the subject of the second independent clause, not the second object of the verb in the first clause. The ambiguity is removed by the following punctuation:

> *The upper limb parallels the clavicle, and the lower limb parallels the fourth interspace.*

What do you think about the next sentence?

> *Local Peyer patch involvement accompanied by severe toxemia and high fever can occur in untreated cases.*

The sentence above is punctuated correctly. You should have recognized that this sentence consists of a single independent clause: the subject is *involvement* and the predicate is *can occur in untreated cases.* The participial phrase *accompanied by severe toxemia and high fever* modifies and restricts the meaning of the subject. Therefore, no internal punctuation is indicated.

EXCEPTION: When a sentence with two independent clauses joined by a coordinating conjunction starts with an introductory phrase (or a dependent clause) that applies to both independent clauses, do <u>not</u> use a comma to separate the two independent clauses if doing so would make the introductory phrase seem to apply only to the first independent clause. In the following sentence, the opening prepositional phrase applies to both independent clauses (the two clauses follow the comma and are separated from each other by the coordinating conjunction *and*).

> *In adoptive-transfer experiments and in the neutralization experiments, the number of effector cells in relation to the number of tumor cells is critical and there seems to be a threshold for the number of effector cells needed to kill a given number of tumor cells.*

I hope that analyzing these sentences has helped you see how the rule calling for a comma to separate independent clauses joined by a coordinating conjunction becomes easier to apply once you have identified the types of phrases and clauses that appear in a sentence.

Items in a series

Before the final "and"

The comma that is used before the final *and* in a **series** is known as the **serial comma.** A series may consist of three or more words, phrases, or clauses. For example, consider the sentence *The specimen was taken from the patient, cultured in the laboratory, and studied microscopically.* In this sentence, the three verbs *taken, cultured,* and *studied* constitute the series. Use of the serial comma varies according to style preferences and the nature of the written material. For example, the Associated Press (AP) does not dictate the use of the serial comma except in more complex sentences; therefore, we do not always find this comma in newspapers and magazines that follow AP style. In biomedical material, however, we must use this comma to prevent ambiguity and confusion. The AMA and CBE style manuals both call for the use of the serial comma. At a dinner several years ago, as I was struggling to explain to a skeptical tablemate why the serial comma was so important, Norman Grossblatt, an AMWA colleague, rescued me by quietly writing the following book inscription on his napkin:

> *To my parents, Ayn Rand and God*

I'm sure you can see the problem caused by omitting the serial comma in this possibly apocryphal inscription. The use of only a single comma has turned *Ayn Rand and God* into an appositive that names the author's parents. Enough said on that one!

Let's look at more examples of sentences that contain series. The following sentence uses the serial comma correctly:

> *When facial components are to be moved surgically, a working knowledge of cephalometric points, planes, angles, and distances is needed for planning the most aesthetic position of the components.*

This is a straightforward example in which the author enumerates four elements that must be considered in planning this procedure. The serial comma is needed to help the reader recognize them clearly and quickly as four discrete elements. Note that when the elements in a series consist of more than single words, the same rule applies: thus, the modified noun *cephalometric points* is an element in the series.

Are the following sentences punctuated correctly? If not, make the changes needed.

> *Three principal bone cells are the osteoblast, the osteocyte and the osteoclast.*

The three complements in this sentence (*the osteoblast, the osteocyte,* and *the osteoclast*) constitute a series. A comma should precede the conjunction *and*:

> *Three principal bone cells are the osteoblast, the osteocyte, and the osteoclast.*

Now try the next sentence. Can you identify the grammatical function of the series in the sentence?

> *This rectangular flap is based medially on the second, third and fourth perforating branches of the internal mammary artery.*

In this sentence, the elements in the series (*the second, third, and fourth perforating branches*) are the objects of the preposition *on.* Again, a comma belongs before the word *and*:

> *This rectangular flap is based medially on the second, third, and fourth perforating branches of the internal mammary artery.*

How would you analyze the next sentence? What is the role of the series here, and how should it be punctuated?

> *Characteristically, the patient is a smoker who has fair skin, a light hair color, and blue or gray eyes.*

The series in the sentence above is the object of the verb *has* in the relative clause that modifies the *smoker.* The sentence is punctuated properly.

The following sentence consists of three independent clauses. These clauses also qualify as a series and call for a serial comma before the *and* preceding the final clause.

> *One patient had a small left ventricle, one patient had a patent foramen ovale, and one patient had anteroseptal akinesis.*

Sometimes a series of three or more modifiers should not be separated by commas because the modifiers are seen as a single term or entity (Iverson, p. 202). Consider the following example:

> *The meal included toast, cereal, and ham and eggs.*

No comma is needed before *and eggs* because *ham and eggs* is treated as a single unit. As the final element in the series, the entire term *and ham and eggs* is preceded properly by a serial comma. We'll see other examples in the following discussion on coordinate adjectives.

Between coordinate adjectives that modify the same noun

Coordinate adjectives may be two or more adjectives, each of which precedes and modifies the same noun. When we are confronted with a series of adjectives all of which modify the same noun, the rules become a little trickier and less rigid. Such adjectives have been separated traditionally by commas, as in the following examples:

> *Dr. Smith is a dedicated, caring physician.*

> *The physician assistant's complicated, impersonal, and incorrect explanation frustrated the patient.*

Be certain that the modifiers do really modify the noun and that none of them modify modifiers. You can most easily identify coordinate adjectives by attempting to reverse their order. Another test you can use for detecting coordinate adjectives is to insert an *and* between the modifiers and see whether the expression retains its meaning:

> *bright, enthusiastic student*

> **BUT** *sleepy medical student*

The modifiers *bright* and *enthusiastic* above qualify as coordinate adjectives because their order could be reversed (*enthusiastic, bright student*) and because the word *and* could be used between them (*bright and enthusiastic student*). In contrast, *sleepy* and *medical* cannot be reversed because *medical sleepy student* or *sleepy and medical student* makes no sense.

If the order of three or more modifying adjectives can be rearranged without affecting the meaning, a comma is generally inserted between them:

> *The extremely hostile, ill-tempered, and dangerously out-of-control patient challenged the staff.*

> *The group conducted a randomized, double-blind, placebo-controlled trial.*

The AMA style manual advises that in some situations a series of three or more modifiers "should not be separated by commas as the modifiers are seen as one term or entity" (Iverson, p. 202) and offers the following examples:

> *chronic progressive multiple sclerosis*

> *inner-city geriatric hemodialysis patients*

The AMA style manual adds a final note that when fewer than three modifiers are used, a comma should <u>not</u> be added if the modifiers and the noun are read as a single entity. The manual provides the following examples (Iverson, p. 202):

a randomized placebo-controlled trial

multicenter clinical trials

Remember to use the comma if the order of the adjectives can be rearranged. Handling multiple modifiers sometimes leaves room for judgment calls. Whichever way you decide to punctuate them for clarity, try to do it consistently.

Opening or ending clauses and phrases

Use a comma when introductory phrases or clauses begin with a subordinating conjunction (eg, *if, although, because, since, when, where, whereas, while*), when they are long, or when confusion would result if they were not set off.

The following example is a complex sentence, containing one dependent clause (the introductory clause underlined) and one independent clause. Opening dependent clauses should be separated by a comma from the independent clause that follows.

<u>Because the infection is chronic</u>, an increase in the concentration of antibodies in the plasma is not useful for diagnosis.

The next sentence opens with the underlined prepositional phrase. A comma is needed after the participle *described* to prevent readers from reading mistakenly "the patient described a lip-splitting incision" and then wondering how *could be made* fits into the sentence. The comma removes the potential confusion by separating the opening phrase from the independent clause (*a lip-splitting incision could be made*).

<u>For the patient described</u>, a lip-splitting incision could be made.

The next sentence would be awkward without a comma before the independent clause:

<u>Whenever appropriate</u>, more than one procedure is discussed.

The opening phrase modifies the verb *is discussed* but appears at the opposite end of the sentence. If you think of this modifier as the dependent clause it implies (Whenever *it is* appropriate), using a comma to separate this opening phrase from the independent clause makes perfect sense and follows the rule. Such phrases are called "elliptical" because essential words are omitted.

As a general rule, use a comma after all introductory prepositional phrases. In the next sentence, potential confusion would result if the opening prepositional phrase were not separated by a comma from the independent clause. Readers could read "In all 18 samples," come to the verb, and have to backtrack to get the clear sense of the sentence.

<u>In all</u>, 18 samples were studied.

When an introductory phrase or clause is transposed to the end of a sentence, a comma might not be needed, depending on whether the phrase is restrictive (essential) or nonrestrictive (nonessential). In the example below, the underlined clause restricts the meaning of the verb by answering the important question *why*, so no comma is used when the phrase is moved to the end of the sentence.

> *Because the venous access line contained heparin*, *the results of the coagulation tests were misleading.*

BUT

> *The results of the coagulation tests were misleading because the venous access line contained heparin*.

Contrasting expressions

The next two examples show how the contrasting expressions *not difficult* and *not the nurse* should be separated from the rest of the sentence.

> *The procedure was easy, not difficult.*
>
> *The IV was started by the resident, not the nurse.*

USING COMMAS TO SET OFF

Now we'll turn to the use of commas to set off various types of words or expressions in a sentence. These functions cover two broad categories:

- Interrupting elements
- Transitional expressions and independent comments

Interrupting elements

Unless they occur at the end of a sentence, nonessential (or nonrestrictive) interrupting elements are usually set off by two commas, one on either side. When these elements are essential to the meaning of the sentence, they should not be set off by commas. Interrupting elements include appositives, dependent clauses, participial phrases, **asides**, degrees, terms of address, years in complete dates, and state names after cities.

Appositives

Remember from Chapter 1 that an appositive is "a noun or noun phrase that identifies another noun or pronoun that immediately precedes it" (Sabin, p. 636). Use a pair of commas to set off a nonrestrictive appositive from the rest of the sentence:

> *George P. Butcher III, MD, an eminent cardiovascular surgeon, will speak after dinner.*
>
> *My physician, Dr. Smith, always responds promptly.*
>
> *This procedure, a standard therapy, is almost always effective.*

BUT do not use a comma when the appositive is essential to the sense of the sentence:

> *Organisms belonging to the genus* Micrococcus *are coagulase negative.*

In the sentence above, the name of the genus (*Micrococcus*) restricts the meaning of the sentence to that genus but no others. Therefore, no comma is used.

> *Sir William Osler is the author of the historic textbook* The Principles and Practice of Medicine.

Osler wrote other books besides *The Principles and Practice of Medicine*. This appositive title restricts the meaning of the sentence by telling us which of his books is being discussed. Again, no comma is used.

Sometimes you will encounter appositives that appear in a sentence in such a way that confusion results. For example,

> *Dr. Stratton, my resident, and I will begin rounds now.*

Exactly how many physicians will there be? Two (Dr. Stratton and I)? Or three (Dr. Stratton, my resident, and I)? The sentence structure is confusing, and the commas surrounding *my resident* do not clarify the confusion. We have several options for correcting this problem.

One option would be to use a different punctuation mark. If Dr. Stratton is your resident, this nonessential appositive would be better set off by placement within **parentheses:** "*Dr. Stratton (my resident) and I will. . . .*" Another option would be to recast the appositive into a relative clause that modifies Dr. Stratton: ie, "*Dr. Stratton, who is my resident, and I will. . . .*" Either of these two options would indicate clearly that two physicians will begin rounds.

If indeed Dr. Stratton is another colleague and three physicians are involved, I suggest rewording the sentence to avoid any possibility of confusion: "*Dr. Stratton and I, along with my resident, will. . . .*" or "*Dr. Stratton, my resident Dr. Jones, and I will. . . .*" In this last rewording, the resident is given a name, which is treated as a restrictive appositive. This restrictive information is not set off by a pair of commas but merely separated by a serial comma from the *and* that introduces the final element in the series.

Dependent clauses

A dependent clause depends on the rest of the sentence to complete its meaning and cannot stand alone. We have already discussed the use of a comma to separate opening dependent clauses. When nonrestrictive dependent clauses occur within a sentence, they should be set off by a pair of commas. In the following sentence, the underlined dependent clause is set off by commas because it is nonrestrictive: that is, the clause could be removed without changing the meaning of the sentence.

> *The patient, although she reported no symptoms, had abnormal signs on her chest radiograph.*

The dependent clause in the next sentence modifies the verb phrase *should begin to recover* by specifying when. When this adverbial clause occurs at the beginning of the sentence, a comma is used. When the adverbial clause follows the main clause, use a comma only if the information is nonrestrictive; in this sentence, the adverbial clause restricts the meaning of the sentence and should <u>not</u> be separated from the main clause.

> <u>*When the therapy has been completed*</u>*, the patient should begin to recover.*

BUT

> *The patient should begin to recover <u>when the therapy has been completed</u>.*

Another type of dependent clause is a relative clause, a clause introduced by a relative pronoun (eg, *that, which, who, whom*) and referring or relating to an antecedent. Let's review what we learned about restrictive and nonrestrictive clauses in Chapter 1. Within or at the end of a sentence, nonrestrictive relative clauses are set off from the rest of the sentence by commas; restrictive clauses are not set off by commas. In the first sentence below, the relative clause modifies the subject (*Bruce*). As a nonrestrictive clause, which could be dropped without destroying the sense of the sentence, the clause is set off by commas:

> *Gordon C. Bruce, Jr, MD, PhD, <u>who conducted the preliminary studies</u>, participated also in the drug's development.*

A clearly restrictive example shows the relative clause at the end of the sentence:

> *The hospital will no longer treat patients <u>who are not covered by insurance</u>.*

The next sentence could go either way, depending upon the context. First, the sentence is shown as having a nonrestrictive relative clause:

> *The disease, <u>which the doctors found difficult to diagnose</u>, did not respond to treatment.*

Suppose, however, that the doctors treated several diseases, but only one disease failed to respond. Then the relative clause would be introduced by the relative pronoun *that*, rather than *which*, and would not be set off with commas:

> *The disease <u>that the doctors found difficult to diagnose</u> did not respond to treatment.*

Distinguishing between nonrestrictive and restrictive material helps us achieve the precision needed in medical writing. If we are editing another author's work and are unsure whether the material is restrictive, we should query the author so that our punctuation will accurately support the meaning intended.

Participial and prepositional phrases

When a participial or prepositional phrase occurs at the beginning of a clause within a compound-complex sentence (two or more independent clauses and at least one dependent clause), handle the comma as if the phrase were an introductory element at the beginning of the sentence. Thus, the participial phrase *viewing the offer as her last resort* is treated as an introductory phrase in the following sentence:

> *The patient was offered participation in a protocol, and <u>viewing the offer as her last resort</u>, she chose to enter the program.*

When participial and prepositional phrases occur at points other than the beginning of a sentence or a clause, the rules for comma use in restrictive or nonrestrictive matter usually apply, as shown in the following sentences:

> *The slide showed blast cells, <u>depicted in Figure 1</u>.* (nonrestrictive participial phrase)
>
> *The recruitment <u>of a new hospital administrator</u> is still underway.* (restrictive prepositional phrase)
>
> *Only one test animal, <u>showing no signs of distress</u>, died before the study was concluded.* (participial phrase, punctuated here as nonrestrictive)

Transitional expressions and independent comments

Still other words and expressions that can interrupt the sentence structure should be set off by commas. **Transitional expressions** (eg, *and so forth, consequently, for example, furthermore, however, in addition, nonetheless, therefore,* and *thus*) serve to support the flow of text by relating preceding material to what will follow. Note that the catchall abbreviation *etc* for the Latin *et cetera*, meaning *and others*, has no place in formal, precise, scientific writing. Its meaning should be spelled out. When *etc* is used (as an abbreviation or spelled out), it should never follow a series of items introduced by *for example, including*, or *eg*, all of which imply already that the list may not be all-inclusive.

> *Covering the cost of bone marrow transplants is, <u>however</u>, difficult.*
>
> *The meeting will be held, <u>nonetheless</u>, on Monday, August 29, 2005, at 9:30 AM in the Surgery Conference Room.*
>
> *Because of the patient's unstable condition, the elective surgery has, <u>of course</u>, been delayed.*

When the coordinating conjunctions *and, but, or, for,* and *nor* are used as transitional expressions at the beginning of a sentence, do not insert a comma directly after the coordinating conjunction (Sabin, p. 29; see also the section "After coordinating conjunctions" later in this chapter):

> <u>*But*</u> *to continue therapy would have been a mistake.*

USING COMMAS TO INDICATE OMISSION OR TO CLARIFY

Next we turn to the third main function of the comma. Using commas to indicate omission or to clarify sometimes requires a little more judgment because variations in sentence structure may be involved. Let's take a closer look at these uses.

Elliptical constructions

A comma is used to indicate omission or to avoid repetition when the sense of the sentence is clear. An **elliptical construction** is a phrasing from which one or more words have been purposely omitted because they can be readily inferred. Parallel structure often supports elliptical constructions. The following examples show how commas are used to indicate omitted material:

> *In the first 2 years, the students study basic science; in the next 2 years, clinical medicine.*
>
> *The most common herbal products used by non-HIV patients were chamomile (13.7%) and aloe vera (8.0%); by HIV patients, chamomile (19.2%) and hibiscus (8.2%).*
>
> *Transesophageal echocardiography (TEE) correctly identified 14 aortic injuries: 5 were confirmed by aortography; 7, by thoracotomy; and 2, by autopsy.*

In the first sentence above, the comma makes it unnecessary to repeat the words *the students study*. The second sentence removes repetition of both the subject and the linking verb. In the third sentence, the words *were confirmed by* are implied rather than being repeated twice.

Unusual word order

As for unusual word order, when clauses or phrases occur out of normal order and when connecting words may be omitted, use a comma to mark the resulting break in the flow of the sentence. For formal writing, *The Gregg Reference Manual* recommends recasting sentences into normal word order (Sabin, p. 38). Consider the following examples:

> *Whatever instructions the professor gives, the student must follow.*
> **Better:** *The student must follow whatever instructions the professor gives.*
>
> *That they should have performed a biopsy, they decided too late.*
> **Better:** *They decided too late that they should have performed a biopsy.*

Many other rules (and exceptions) indicating the use of commas can be found in a good style manual. The Bibliography in this module lists a number of such manuals. This chapter discusses the rules that should be most relevant for your work; the intent is not to overwhelm you with every existing rule and exception. Once you master the application of these basic rules and arm yourself with relevant style manuals, you should have much greater confidence in your ability to use the comma appropriately.

WHEN <u>NOT</u> TO USE A COMMA

The final section of this chapter addresses situations in which a comma should <u>not</u> be used. In these situations, the comma serves only to confuse the reader

---

Do <u>not</u> use a comma

- ◆ To separate a subject from its verb or a verb from its object or complement
- ◆ To separate a coordinating conjunction from the following word

Please do not underestimate the value of this final section. Many writers err quite consistently by inserting commas that separate elements that belong together. When <u>not</u> to use a comma is every bit as important as when <u>to</u> use one.

The main rules prohibiting comma usage are neither difficult nor numerous. Let's review them now.

RULE: Do NOT use a comma to separate a subject from its verb or a verb from its object or complement.

We have already learned that a compound sentence consists of two or more independent clauses joined by a coordinating conjunction and that a comma is usually needed before the conjunction, unless the clauses to be joined are very short and the meaning of the sentence would be perfectly clear without the comma. For purposes of review, the following examples demonstrate the application of this rule.

In the sentence below, a comma separates correctly the two independent clauses joined by a coordinating conjunction:

> *Osteoradionecrosis is the most dreaded complication, and osteotomy sites are always areas of concern.*

The next sentence has short clauses and is clear without a comma:

> *The hospital is downtown and transportation is readily available.*

Compound subjects

Study the following sentence and analyze its elements. Then decide what, if any, punctuation is needed and why.

> *Important advances in the vocal rehabilitation of patients after total laryngectomy and improved techniques for laryngeal reconstruction after partial laryngectomy have caused us to revise our thinking about the role of surgery.*

This sentence has a compound subject. Both subjects, *important advances* and *improved techniques*, are modified by prepositional phrases that follow them. The verb in the sentence is *have caused.* And the rule tells us not to use a comma to separate a subject from its verb. Therefore, no comma should be used in the sentence.

Likewise, a comma should not separate an adjective from the noun that follows it: eg, *competent nurses*, NOT *competent, nurses.*

Compound predicates

A predicate is the part of the sentence that states what the subject does, what is done to the subject, or what the subject's state of being is. In other words, the predicate consists of the verb and its object or its complement, when a linking verb is used. A sentence with two or more predicates joined by a conjunction has a compound predicate; as a general rule, a comma should not be used to separate the two predicates:

> *The preliminary report covers findings from laboratory animals and awaits the results of clinical trials.*

The subject of this sentence is *The preliminary report*. Can you identify the two verbs? You should have identified *covers* and *awaits*: the report both covers something and awaits something. The rule tells us not to separate a subject from its verb or verbs. Therefore, a comma should not be used in this sentence. What happens if we insert a comma before the conjunction *and*, which links the two predicates?

> *The preliminary report covers findings from laboratory animals, and awaits the results of clinical trials.*

By inserting the comma, we signal the reader that a complete independent clause will follow; however, what follows (*and awaits the results of clinical trials*) is not an independent clause because it has no subject.

One way to think about comma usage when compound predicates are involved is well stated in the AMA style manual:

> . . . be careful not to confuse a coordinating conjunction used to link a compound predicate with the coordinating conjunction used between independent clauses (Iverson, p. 203).

The Gregg Reference Manual expresses the same point in a slightly different way:

> Do not confuse a compound sentence with a simple sentence containing a compound predicate (Sabin, p. 17).

The advice in these quotations will go a long way toward helping you to write with greater clarity.

Now that you thoroughly understand compound predicates and why commas are generally not used to separate a subject from its verbs, I have to throw you a curve: unfortunately, sometimes you must make an exception! The following sentence is an example:

> *The complex nature of this regulated assembly provides virtually unlimited possibilities for regulation, and results in a fail-safe mechanism for controlling gene expression.*

This sentence uses a comma between the compound verbs *provides* and *results*. Can you see a reason for breaking the rule not to use a comma? If the sentence did not contain the comma, the reader might first read this as "possibilities for regulation and [for] results," because *results* can be not only a verb but also a noun. For the sake of clarity and to prevent readers from having to stop in their tracks until they realize that *results* is functioning here as a verb rather than as the second object of the preposition *for*, we make an exception and insert the comma. Clarity is the overriding justification for this exception, as for most exceptions.

Objects and complements

Within a predicate, a transitive verb may have compound objects. The object is whatever receives the action of the verb and may be a word, a phrase, or a clause. The complement completes the sense of a linking verb. The rule that applies to multiple objects and complements is parallel to the rule that applies to subject and verbs in compound predicates:

RULE: Do not use a comma to separate a verb from its objects or complements.

Consider the following examples:

> *The remodeled laboratory contains state-of-the-art lighting and the newest equipment.*

The example above is a simple sentence with two modified objects, *lighting* and *equipment*. Clearly, no comma is needed between *lighting* and the conjunction *and*.

> *The Austin Appeals Court's mention of the "zone of danger" was a side issue and not binding on lower courts as precedent.*

The two complements in the second example are *a side issue* and *not binding on lower courts*; both complete the sense of the verb *was*, and a comma should not be used before the *and* that links them.

After coordinating conjunctions

RULE: Do NOT use a comma to separate a coordinating conjunction from the following word.

The following example is <u>incorrect</u>:

> *We conclude (1) that residents perform well on structured clinical examinations, (2) that they prefer these examinations to multiple-choice tests, and, (3) that they consider such examinations a learning experience.*

Even without the parenthetic numerals (a deletion that AMA style would consider preferable), the comma after *and* in the second line is incorrect. A comma is acceptable after a coordinating conjunction only when a transitional expression interrupts the flow of the sentence and needs to be set off by a pair of commas:

> *The Austin Appeals Court's mention of the "zone of danger" was a side issue and, <u>therefore</u>, not binding on lower courts as precedent.*

Styles for the use of commas in numerals

Styles vary regarding the use of commas in numerals. The AMA style follows the International System of Units (SI) convention, making the decimal point the only punctuation mark used in numerals. A 4-digit number is solid (*7562*), and the digits in larger whole numbers are separated by half-spaces into groups of three (Iverson, p. 484):

1234	*123.456*	*1 234 567*
12 345	*123.4567*	*1 234 5678.8*
123 456	*123.456 78*	

Although a comma is placed between the day and the year in a complete date, no comma is used when only the month and the year are written:

> *July 24, 2006*
>
> **BUT** *July 2006*

Not all publications follow these practices, so always check the style called for by the publication for which you are writing.

Many more rules for comma usage exist; however, our purpose here is cover the rules needed to handle the most basic punctuation challenges you are likely to encounter. When no rule seems to apply, you might read the sentence aloud to find distinct pauses that may need commas. Developing the habit of analyzing sentences and identifying their elements, as we have done throughout this chapter, should enable you to apply these rules appropriately and to locate additional rules, as needed, in style manuals.

1. **Federal law allows states to set standards that must be at least as strict as federal standards and, the EPA approves and oversees these state programs.**

   Which of the following best describes the punctuation in this sentence?

   a. No comma is needed.
   b. The comma is not placed correctly.
   c. The comma separates correctly two independent clauses joined by a coordinating conjunction.

2. **In all of the studies above the primary endpoint will be survival.**

   What punctuation does this sentence need?

   a. a comma after *all*.
   b. a comma after *above*.
   c. a comma to separate *studies* and *above* to prevent ambiguity.
   d. a comma to separate the introductory clause from the independent clause.

3. **Protein translation is determined by the availability of the corresponding amino acids and by the activity of specific aminoacyl-tRNA synthetases, the overall rate of protein synthesis and other factors.**

   What punctuation does this sentence need?

   a. no changes.
   b. a comma after *amino acids*.
   c. a comma before *and other factors*.

4. **As exposure to the offending agent continues more and more bronchial damage develops, accompanied by irreversible changes occurring in the airways.**

   Which of the following best describes the punctuation in this sentence?

   a. The punctuation is correct.
   b. A comma should be placed after *continues*.
   c. A pair of commas should set off *more and more* for clarity.
   d. A comma should not separate an introductory dependent clause from an independent clause.

5. **Conversely less than 5% of cancers are explained by genetics alone, and the remainder are the consequence of the interaction between environmental factors and genetic and acquired susceptibility.**

   What punctuation does this sentence need?

   a. no changes.
   b. a comma between *factors* and the word *and* for the sake of clarity.
   c. a comma to separate the introductory transitional expression from the first independent clause.
   d. removal of the comma between the two independent clauses because they are joined by a coordinating conjunction.

6. **Hospitals in the southwestern United States could also be negatively affected, but appear more prepared to handle the reimbursement cuts.**

   The punctuation in this sentence

   a. is correct.
   b. should not separate the subject from its second verb.
   c. needs a pair of commas to set off the prepositional phrase because it is nonrestrictive and interrupts the flow of the sentence.

7. **Data from returned questionnaires were entered into a database and reviewed subsequently by a person unfamiliar with the questionnaire for accuracy, missing values, outliers, and distribution.**

   This sentence needs

   a. no additional punctuation.
   b. removal of the comma after *outliers*.
   c. a comma separating *database* and the word *and*.

8. **There is no evidence that antibacterial antibodies although present play any role in this acquired immunity.**

   What punctuation does this sentence need?

   a. no changes.
   b. a comma to separate *present* and *play*.
   c. a pair of commas to set off *although present*.
   d. a comma to set off *in this acquired immunity*.

9. **Completing the difficult time-consuming operation, Dr. Hansen rushed back to her patient in the Surgical Intensive Care Unit.**

   Which of the following best describes the punctuation in this sentence?

   a. The sentence is punctuated correctly.
   b. A comma is needed to separate coordinate adjectives.
   c. The comma separating *operation* and *Dr. Hansen* is not necessary for clarity.

The Semicolon (;)

3

As a mark of linkage, the semicolon is weaker than the colon but stronger than the comma. It is a mark of coordination.

—Scientific Style and Format (p. 46)

The semicolon indicates a more definite break in thought than does a comma, "calls for a longer pause in reading," and "is used whenever a comma would not be sufficiently distinctive" (Skillin, p. 182). One of the most useful marks at a writer's disposal, the semicolon suffers from considerable misuse or nonuse. A surprisingly large number of writers, including medical writers, seem to avoid using it altogether, possibly because they don't know the few simple rules that govern its use. Every medical writer should be able to use this mark correctly, with comfort and confidence. Let's look at the rules for using the semicolon.

Use a semicolon

To separate independent clauses
- When they are <u>not</u> joined by a coordinating conjunction
- When main clauses are joined by a conjunctive adverb or by a coordinating conjunction if one of the clauses has internal punctuation or is extremely long

To ensure clarity
- Between items in a complex or lengthy enumeration
- In an enumeration that contains serial commas in at least one item

---

The rules above tell us when to use a semicolon, usually instead of a comma. In this chapter, we will learn how to apply each of these rules.

USE OF THE SEMICOLON WITH INDEPENDENT CLAUSES

To separate independent clauses <u>not</u> joined by a coordinating conjunction

We learned in Chapter 1 that a compound sentence consists of two independent clauses; in Chapter 2, we learned that these two clauses are separated by a comma when they are joined by a coordinating conjunction (such as *and* or *but*). Let's look again at the example used in our discussion of the comma:

> *Fewer Hispanics than whites work in smoke-free environments, and younger workers are less protected than are older workers.*

This sentence consists of two independent clauses, joined by the coordinating conjunction *and* and separated by a comma. If these clauses were <u>not</u> joined by the coordinating conjunction, as shown below, a comma would <u>not</u> be the appropriate punctuation mark in the absence of the conjunction:

> *Fewer Hispanics than whites work in smoke-free environments, younger workers are less protected than are older workers.*

I hope you can see how the incorrectly punctuated sentence above doesn't quite work. Without the conjunction, the comma fails to provide a sufficient break, and the two clauses sound rather choppy and disconnected. The comma just doesn't do the job here. The first rule for use of the semicolon between independent clauses is as follows:

RULE: Use a semicolon to separate independent clauses when no connective word is used.

Replacing the comma with a semicolon shows this rule applied properly:

> *Fewer Hispanics than whites work in smoke-free environments; younger workers are less protected than are older workers.*

The semicolon in the sentence above not only provides a definitive break but also implies that the second clause will be related closely to the first. In this sense, the semicolon serves the dual purpose both of separating and of linking.

Separating the two independent clauses by placing a period after the first clause and making the second clause a new sentence is sometimes an acceptable option; however, if the writer wants to preserve the closer relationship between the two clauses, the semicolon would be the mark of choice.

How would you punctuate the following two independent clauses?

> *Suppressing growth hormone is of particular concern for long-term treatment of children*
>
> *A new pediatric research facility is now on the drawing board*

Let's review our options. A comma would be incorrect because the two clauses are not joined by a coordinating conjunction. A semicolon would be another option, but think about the two clauses—are they really related to each other strongly enough that they belong in the same sentence? I think not. For these two clauses, two separate sentences would be the best choice, reflecting the lack of relationship between the clauses.

In contrast, the two clauses in the sentence below would justify the use of the semicolon because they are both concerned with the subject of the first clause, *suppressing growth hormone*:

> *Suppressing growth hormone is of particular concern for long-term treatment of children; no studies of this subject have been published to date.*

The next example also applies this rule to use a semicolon to separate two main clauses with no coordinating conjunction. In this sentence, the second clause is modified by a participial phrase, separated from the clause with a comma.

> *Interferon protects solid tissues during virus infection; interferon is also disseminated through the bloodstream during viremia, thereby protecting distant organs against the spreading infection.*

EXCEPTION: If two independent clauses are short and parallel in form, a comma may be used.

> *Freshmen attended the lecture, seniors made ward rounds.*

Clarity should be the deciding factor in whether to use a comma or a semicolon between short independent clauses.

To separate main clauses joined by a connective word (a conjunctive adverb or a coordinating conjunction) if one of the clauses has internal punctuation or is lengthy

In sentences with two independent clauses joined by a conjunction, we already know that some relationship exists between the clauses. The next rule explains when a semicolon should be used instead of a comma:

RULE: Use a semicolon between main clauses joined by a conjunctive adverb (eg, *accordingly, also, besides, furthermore, then, however, nevertheless, thus, hence, indeed,* **and** *yet*) **or by a coordinating conjunction if one of the clauses has internal punctuation or is extremely long.**

Note that this rule applies also to expressions like *for example, that is,* and *namely* when a major break in continuity is indicated.

> *The students performed poorly on their board examinations; and it was noted that many had difficulty relating to patients when on rotation, either on the campus or at one of the satellite clinics, through the internal medicine and dermatology services.*

The coordinating conjunction *and* joins the two main clauses in the sentence above. The second clause is interrupted by the nonrestrictive phrase *either on the campus or at one of the satellite clinics,* which is set off by a pair of commas. This internal punctuation in the second clause mandates the use of the semicolon earlier in the sentence.

Now let's consider another version of this sentence:

> *The students performed poorly on their board examinations; furthermore, it was noted that many had difficulty relating to patients when on rotation through the internal medicine and dermatology services.*

The **conjunctive adverb** *furthermore* in the sentence above reinforces the relationship between the two main clauses. Note that conjunctive adverbs used in this manner are followed by a comma.

The next sentence contains three clauses. Can you identify the rules that apply here?

> *The patient's surgery went smoothly; however, her postoperative recovery was complicated by a seizure, and a Neurology consult was requested.*

Analysis of this sentence yields an opening independent clause separated by the semicolon from the conjunctive adverb *however*. This adverb (followed by a comma) introduces two independent clauses (a compound sentence) joined by the coordinating conjunction *and,* with a comma preceding the conjunction and separating these last two clauses.

USE OF THE SEMICOLON IN ENUMERATIONS

We learned in Chapter 2 that commas provide adequate punctuation to separate the elements in reasonably uncomplicated series (eg, *books, magazines, and newspapers*); however, sentences with long, involved enumerations appear often in the medical literature. Without proper punctuation, such enumerations can be confusing. The final section of this chapter presents the conditions under which a semicolon should be used (instead of a comma) to ensure clarity in enumerations.

Between items in a complex or lengthy enumeration

The rule for punctuating complex or lengthy enumerations is as follows:

RULE: Use semicolons between items in a complex or lengthy enumeration within a sentence.

Here is an example:

> *To investigate a new treatment regimen, a randomized phase III trial is superior to a phase II trial because the latter is associated with two statistical concerns: first, the effect of the existing treatment is considered to be a constant reference for comparison, but it is actually an estimate, and its variation is typically ignored; second, patients treated with the new treatment in the current study might differ in important ways from those treated with the existing treatment in past studies.*

In this sentence, the semicolon provides a clear break that helps the reader separate the two statistical concerns.

Now let's consider the punctuation involving a series, which consists of three or more elements.

In an enumeration that contains internal punctuation in at least one item

Often an item in an enumeration contains a series. Following is the rule for punctuation when this is the case:

RULE: Use a semicolon to separate items in an enumeration when at least one item contains internal punctuation.

The sentences that follow apply this rule mandating use of a semicolon to clarify potential confusion:

The Adult Treatment Panel III of the National Cholesterol Education Program identifies specific fasting considerations of LDL cholesterol as optimal and identifies LDL-cholesterol treatment goals based on risk factors that include whether a patient smokes cigarettes; has hypertension, low HDL cholesterol, or a family history of heart disease; and is of a certain age.

Pathologic discharge from the breast is serous, serosanguinous, or bloody; spontaneous rather than produced only by squeezing; persistent; and nonlactational.

The board includes representatives from three key groups within the community: attorneys or judges of good repute; professors of art, literature, or another of the humanities; and the clergy.

In summary, the semicolon is a particularly useful tool for eliminating potential confusion in highly technical and complicated text. The next chapter will focus on an even stronger punctuation mark that serves other, more rhetorical purposes.

Select the answer that best describes the punctuation needed in each of the following sentences.

1. **Smart analysis of STX4A shows three domains: a syntaxin N-terminal domain, which is likely to anchor the protein to the cytoplasmic surface of cellular membranes; a target-SNARE domain, which probably interacts with a cognate vesicle-targeting receptor in vesicles, and a C-terminal transmembrane domain.**

    a. No changes.
    b. A semicolon after *vesicles.*
    c. A comma following *membranes.*
    d. A semicolon after *three domains.*

2. **Heating fresh serum for 15 min at 56°C destroys lytic action and some other functions of complement, therefore heating is frequently used to deactivate complement's activity.**

    a. No changes.
    b. A comma after *therefore.*
    c. A semicolon before *therefore.*
    d. A semicolon before and a comma following *therefore.*

3. **Breast reconstruction provides various benefits for the patient: it avoids the need for an external prosthesis, allows the mastectomy patient freedom to wear almost any kind of clothing, including swimwear; and permits her to exercise without worry about dislodging an external prosthesis.**

    a. No changes.
    b. A semicolon should be placed before *allows.*
    c. The comma before *including* should be deleted.
    d. The colon after *for the patient* should be changed to a semicolon to separate the two independent clauses without a coordinating conjunction.

4. **For lower lip reconstruction, the pedicle is tubed and passed externally; the distal end is folded upon itself and tailored into the defect.**

    a. No comma is needed after the introductory phrase.
    b. A comma would be adequate instead of the semicolon.
    c. A semicolon is used because the two independent clauses are not joined by a conjunctive adverb.
    d. A semicolon is used because the two independent clauses are not joined by a coordinating conjunction.

5. **Both specific antibodies and cytotoxic T lymphocytes are found in the peripheral blood of animals with allergic encephalomyelitis (EAE), but cell-mediated immune responses are most important because EAE is transferred to normal recipients by lymphocytes rather than by serum from diseased animals.**

   a. No changes.
   b. The comma needs to be changed to a semicolon to separate the two independent clauses.
   c. The comma needs to be deleted because the two independent clauses are separated by a coordinating conjunction.

6. **The author was unable to attend all specialty clinic sessions during the study period, thus opportunity biases also may have affected the results.**

   a. No changes.
   b. A comma after *thus.*
   c. A semicolon before and a comma after *thus.*
   d. A semicolon to replace the comma after *period.*

7. **Only one doctor not delivering babies paid more than $33,000. This doctor practiced obstetrics until 1997 and reported that he is still paying for long-term coverage ("tail coverage") of obstetrics. The malpractice premiums were significantly higher for doctors who practiced obstetrics than for doctors who did not.**

   a. No changes.
   b. A semicolon between the first two independent clauses.
   c. A semicolon between the second and third independent clauses.
   d. Semicolons between the first and second and between the second and third independent clauses.

8. **The chin position must be evaluated in both the AP and vertical planes, if a transverse problem is apparent, an additional posteroanterior (PA) skull film analysis is indicated.**

   a. No changes.
   b. A period after *planes.*
   c. A semicolon between *planes* and *if.*
   d. A semicolon between *apparent* and *an.*

The Colon (:)

A colon works like a drumroll: it prepares you for the cymbal's clash;
a semicolon is more like a modulation.
—*Scientific Style and Format (CBE)*, p. 44

The orchestral simile above (attributed to J. S. Allen) is a wonderful way to remember how the colon functions. We learned in Chapter 1 that the colon is a stronger mark than the comma or the semicolon; thus, the colon heralds a strong break. Only the period and other end-of-sentence punctuation marks indicate stronger breaks.

A mark of separation, like the comma and the semicolon, the colon separates grammatical elements. The colon follows a clause and may be placed between clauses. The guideline that simplifies its use (and is most often ignored) follows:

The clause before the colon *must be independent*.

In other words, a clause that could not be a complete sentence should not be followed by a colon. The AMA style manual (p. 206) supports this guideline with two general corollaries indicating "When Not to Use a Colon":

1. **Do <u>not</u> use a colon if the sentence is continuous without it.** Even though the verb *ordered* in the example below introduces a list of three items, the sentence is continuous without a colon.

   The internist ordered a complete blood count, a urinalysis, and an MRI.

The next sentence violates this guideline; the colon after *offer* should be deleted:

INCORRECT: *Professional organizations can and should offer: credible practice guidelines, topical information, and access to continuing education.*

CORRECT: *Professional organizations can and should offer credible practice guidelines, topical information, and access to continuing education.*

2. **Do <u>not</u> use a colon to separate a preposition from its object or a verb (including all forms of the verb *to be*) from its object or complement.** The AMA style manual includes further the admonition to avoid using a colon after *because* or forms of the verb *include*. Can you think of other examples of this erroneous use of the colon?

The sentences below show constructions to avoid. In each one, the colon should have been deleted.

> **AVOID:** *The conference included: lectures, workshops, and poster sessions.*

The colon incorrectly separates the verb *included* from its objects (*lectures, workshops, and poster sessions*).

> **AVOID:** *The rule is: When in doubt, leave it out.*

The colon incorrectly separates the verb *is* from its complement (the stated rule). Punctuated correctly, the sentence would read *The rule is When in doubt, leave it out.* or *The rule is as follows: When in doubt, leave it out.*

> **AVOID:** *Evaluations for treatment-related effects were based on: clinical observations, physical examinations, and gross postmortem examinations.*

In this sentence, the colon incorrectly separates the preposition *on* from the objects *clinical observations, physical examinations, and gross postmortem examinations.*

WHEN TO USE A COLON

Armed with these guidelines for when not to use a colon, let's now learn the rules for using this effective punctuation mark.

> ### Use a colon
>
> ◆ After an independent clause that states or suggests *"the following"*
> ◆ Before lists or to introduce formal quotations
> ◆ Between two independent clauses, the second of which develops, details, or amplifies the first

The uses listed above are not always mutually exclusive, but let's look at each one individually, along with pertinent examples.

After an independent clause that states or suggests *"the following"*

The rule that mandates placing a colon after an independent clause that states explicitly *the following* or *as follows* can be easily applied:

Arthropods that may contribute to allergic respiratory disease are <u>as follows</u>: mayflies, caddis flies, bees, aphids, moths, beetles, Mexican bean weevils, mushroom flies, cockroaches, and microcrustacea.

<u>The following</u> serologic tests have been used to diagnose bunyavirus infections: complement-fixation, fluorescent antibody, hemagglutination-inhibition, and neutralization tests.

The wording *the following* in the sentence above alerts the reader to expect information about specific serologic tests; the colon after the independent clause says, in effect, "Here are the tests!" Can you think of a way to punctuate the same information in a sentence without stating but only suggesting or implying *the following*?

Consider the next two sentences, which imply *the following* but do not actually state it:

In strains of E coli, two types of pili are easily recognized: the short, abundant common pili and a small number (1–6) of very long pili, known as the sex pili.

Serologic tests have been used to diagnose bunyavirus infections: complement-fixation, fluorescent antibody, hemagglutination-inhibition, and neutralization tests.

Although *the following* is not expressed, look carefully at both sentences to see whether it could be inserted. *The following* is implied in both. In fact, the second sentence above meets the criteria for two of the rules for colon use: the words *the following* are suggested, and the colon provides a break before the list of tests. Why does the third rule regarding two independent clauses not apply here?

The rule does not apply because the information following the colon is not an independent clause but merely a series of items with no subject or verb—actually, not a clause at all. We'll look at this rule in more detail shortly.

Before lists or to introduce formal quotations

Elements in a list may be words, phrases, or independent clauses. Some additional examples of the colon used to introduce a list follow:

The larynx performs three important functions (ranked in order of their importance): (1) protection, (2) respiration, and (3) phonation.

Copies of the reports were distributed as follows: to the attending physician on the ward service, to the patient's family, and to the referring physician.

He defined the roles of the principal players: authors must report honestly what they observe, reviewers are consultants to editors, and editors are proxies for readers.

The emergency involved the following measures: Patients who could be moved were evacuated from the facility. Personnel designated as "Essential" were told that after making whatever arrangements were necessary for their families and property they were to bring food and water for 3 days. Once they had reported to the facility, the essential personnel were expected to remain there until the crisis had passed.

Also, the colon may be used to introduce a formal or extended quotation <u>when the colon follows an independent clause.</u>

Today's physicians would do well to remember Osler's famous words of wisdom: "The practice of medicine is an art, not a trade; a calling, not a business; a calling in which your heart will be exercised equally with your head."

His words are often cited: "Advice is sought to confirm a position already taken."

Irby, in delineating legal guidelines for dismissing medical students, has underscored this reluctance on the part of faculty to point out problems: "Only in extreme cases," he says, "have faculty been willing to make negative evaluations."

Note that when the quoted material "comes at the end of a sentence and is introduced by an expression such as *he said* or *she said*, a comma usually precedes the opening quotation mark" (Sabin, p. 73); but if the quotation contains more than one sentence, use a colon:

After the students failed to notice the patient's affect, the professor said wearily, "None are so blind as those who have eyes and see not."

One student replied, "But, Dr. Browning, I did notice that the patient's affect was flat."

BUT: *Again, Osler said: "Live a simple and a temperate life, that you may give all your powers to your profession. Medicine is a jealous mistress; she will be satisfied with no less."*

The final example above uses a colon, not a comma, because the quotation consists of more than one sentence.

Between two independent clauses, the second of which develops, details, or amplifies the first

We learned in Chapter 3 that a semicolon can be used to separate two related independent clauses that are not joined by a coordinating conjunction; however, when the second independent clause explains or amplifies the first clause, a colon is the more effective punctuation mark. Thus, the relationship between the two clauses determines whether to use a semicolon, a colon, or a period. In the examples below, which use colons, the second clause amplifies or explains the first clause:

The surgery professor has a busy schedule on Wednesday: she must perform three operations in the morning, make ward rounds with the students, attend a faculty luncheon meeting, deliver a lecture, and attend two more committee meetings.

The family members of the patient are responding as we expected: right now, they are denying the seriousness of his condition.

Which of the following versions of the same information most clearly makes the point? Can you explain the difference each punctuation mark makes in the sentence?

1. *Smoke-free policies are strongly correlated with age, with younger workers reporting reporting lower levels of these policies than middle-aged and older workers.*

2. *Smoke-free policies are strongly correlated with age; younger workers report lower levels of these policies than do middle-aged and older workers.*

3. *Smoke-free policies are strongly correlated with age: younger workers report lower levels of these policies than do middle-aged and older workers.*

You should have recognized that Sentence 1 above has only one independent clause; the information supporting that clause is presented in a modifying phrase, which lessens the impact of the information. The next two sentences have been reworded to recast the modifying phrase into a second independent clause, making a crisper, cleaner sentence. Sentence 2 uses the semicolon correctly, but the use of the colon in Sentence 3 is more effective because this mark signals to the reader that a fuller explanation of the first clause is forthcoming. Remember the drumroll analogy!

OTHER USES FOR THE COLON

The colon performs several additional functions; those most relevant are mentioned briefly below.

In expressions of time

Use a colon to separate hours from minutes in an expression of time:

Blood was drawn daily at 7:30 AM, at 12:30 PM, and at 7:30 PM.

In expressions of numerical ratios

Use a colon to separate the parts of numerical ratios.

The ratio of T4 to T8 lymphocytes is 1:4.

The normal HbA$_1$:HbA$_2$ ratio is 40:1.

In bibliographic references

In journal article references, the colon has two uses: the first, to separate a title from a subtitle; the second, to separate the volume (and issue) number from the page numbers:

Serruys PW, Kutryk MJB, Ong ATL. Drug therapy: coronary-artery stents. *N Engl J Med.* 2006;354(5):483–495.

In references to books, a colon is used to separate the name (usually abbreviated) of the state or country where the book was published from the name of the publisher:

Schwager E. *Medical English Usage and Abusage.* Phoenix, AZ: Oryx Press; 1991.

If a chapter in a multiauthor text is being cited, a colon separates the year of publication from the page numbers. As shown below, colons separate the following elements:

- The title from the subtitle of the chapter
- "*In*" from the name of the book editor
- The title from the subtitle of the book
- The state abbreviation from the publisher
- The year from the inclusive page numbers

[handwritten annotation: & volume (and issue) from first page]

Kantoff PW, Talcott JA. The prostate specific antigen: its use as a tumor marker for prostate cancer. In: Hayes DF, ed. *Hematology/Oncology Clinics of North America: Tumor Markers in Adult Solid Malignancies.* Philadelphia, PA: WB Saunders; 1997:1502–1539.

Note that titles of books and journals are set in italics.

PUNCTUATION FOR VERTICAL LISTS FOLLOWING A COLON

Forthcoming chapters will discuss rules for punctuation when colons are placed next to certain other punctuation marks in a sentence. But before we leave our discussion of the colon, you may find rules for punctuating vertical lists helpful. We see vertical lists punctuated every which way: with semicolons separating the items, with commas, with no punctuation, and with the added flourish of a coordinating conjunction before the final item. At the very least, consistency is a virtue here; however, easy-to-follow rules are even better. So if you have been searching all your life (as I did) for simple rules covering punctuation for vertical lists, you may find the following guidance helpful (Woolever, pp. 478–480).

If elements are incomplete sentences (phrases or words)

A clause must comprise three elements:

- *Subject*
- *Verb*
- *Object (if verb is transitive) or complement*

Use NO commas, NO serial "and," and NO period.

If an element contains one or more complete sentences

Blood samples were tested for the following:

- *Prothrombin time (PT).*
- *Activated partial thromboplastin time (aPTT).*
- *von Willebrand Factor (vWF). A sample must usually be sent to a reference laboratory for this measurement.*
- *Complete blood count (CBC).*

Place a period after each list element.

Note: You should know that the guidelines above (and used in this module) differ from the style used in the AMA style manual. The one example of a vertical enumeration in the AMA manual (Iverson, p. 517) shows semicolons at the end of each item and a period after the final item. Neither Woolever nor AMA uses a coordinating conjunction before the final item. Because I like the logic of Woolever's rules, I have presented them above for your consideration if you are not bound to use the semicolons and period.

This concludes our discussion of the colon. Chapters 2 through 4 have covered the main punctuation marks that separate the grammatical elements <u>within</u> a sentence: commas, semicolons, and colons. Now we are ready to learn about other marks that punctuate our writing.

1. **Clinics surveyed for the study were: endocrinology, neurology, cardiology, otorlaryngology, and nephrology.**

   Which answer best describes correct punctuation in this sentence?

   a. No changes are needed.
   b. The colon should be deleted.
   c. The colon is used to introduce an enumeration.
   d. The items in the series should be separated by semicolons.

2. **Our basic approach involved three steps ___ first, we adopted estimates from HCFA for the years that they are available; second, we generated estimates using our own methods and data sources; and third, we adjusted our estimates for the years not covered by HCFA to reflect differences between the HCFA figures and our figures for the years that both are available.**

   Which punctuation mark will best serve in the blank space above?

   a. A colon.
   b. A period.
   c. A comma.
   d. A semicolon.

3. **George Lundberg, MD, speaking at an AMWA annual conference, made this profound observation; "The road to senility is paved with plaques."**

   Which answer best describes correct punctuation for this sentence?

   a. No changes are needed.
   b. A comma should introduce the quotation.
   c. A semicolon separates two independent clauses.
   d. A colon should be used to introduce the quotation.

4. **The holiday shopping season illustrates the high-end concentration of spending __ retailers that cater to lower- and middle-income shoppers had disappointing results, whereas the luxury chains thrived.**

   Which punctuation mark is needed in the blank space above?

   a. A colon.
   b. A period.
   c. A comma.
   d. A semicolon.

5. **Grundy SM, Hansen B, Smith SC, et al: Clinical management of the metabolic syndrome. *Circulation.* 2004;109:551–556.**

   Which answer would describe correct punctuation (according to AMA style) for this reference?

   a. No changes are needed.
   b. A colon should separate the list of authors from the title.
   c. A colon should separate the year from the volume number.
   d. A colon should separate the volume number from the page numbers.

6. **Physicians are knowledgeable about the implications of: malnutrition, cigarette smoking, and heavy drinking.**

   Which answer best describes correct punctuation in this sentence?

   a. No changes are needed.
   b. The colon after *of* introduces the enumeration.
   c. The colon between *of* and *malnutrition* should be deleted.
   d. The items in the series should be separated by semicolons.

7. **The committee required applicants to submit specific credentials and documentation __ an essay describing the applicant's education, experience, and interests; school transcripts; and two letters of recommendation.**

   Which punctuation mark is needed in the blank space above?

   a. A colon.
   b. A period.
   c. A comma.
   d. A semicolon.

8. **Seventy-five patients met the criteria for the study __ 66 chose to participate.**

   Which punctuation mark is needed in the blank space above?

   a. A colon.
   b. A period.
   c. A comma.
   d. A semicolon.

9. **The patients who declined chose not to participate because __ the study would involve too much of their time, they didn't want to receive the placebo, and frequent transportation to the hospital for follow-up was a problem for them.**

   Which punctuation mark is needed in the blank space above?

   a. None.
   b. A colon.
   c. A comma.
   d. A semicolon.

10. **As of June 15, 2005, CDC had antigenically characterized 1024 influenza viruses collected by US laboratories since the October 2003 report; 949 influenza A (H3N2) viruses, three influenza A (H1) viruses, one influenza A (H7N2) virus, and 71 influenza B viruses.**

    Which answer describes the correct punctuation in this sentence?

    a. No changes are needed.
    b. A dash should be used after *report*.
    c. A colon should replace the semicolon.
    d. The semicolon correctly separates the two main clauses.

11. **The three elements—X, XX, and XXX—were mixed in a ratio of _____.**

    Which of the following will serve best in the blank space above?

    a. 4-2-1.
    b. 4:2:1.
    c. 4 to 2 to 1.

Dashes (—, –)

**Less formal than the comma or the colon,
the dash should be used sparingly.**
—Author unknown

Dashes serve to indicate a break in the thought or structure of a sentence. We have already seen how commas, semicolons, and colons separate elements within a sentence; now we will learn how and when use of the **dash** is appropriate. "Dashes as another form of internal punctuation convey a particular meaning or emphasize and clarify a certain section of material" (Iverson, p. 213).

Four different types of dashes are distinguished from each other by their length and their functions:

- The em dash, equal to the width of the capital letter "M"
- The **en dash,** equal to the width of the capital letter "N"
- The two-em dash
- The three-em dash

The em dash and the en dash are the two types used most often. Most computer keyboards do not have a separate key for each of these marks; however, they can be formed in several ways.

On your keyboard, an em dash can be formed between two words by typing two hyphens with no spacing on either side; the em dash appears after you place a space after the second word.

Both the em dash and the en dash can be found and inserted from Symbols under the Insert menu in Microsoft Word.

Still another way to produce these two dashes uses the number pad:

- Em dash—press CTRL + ALT keys + the hyphen key on the number pad
- En dash—press CTRL key + the hyphen key on the number pad

THE EM DASH

By far the most commonly used dash, the em dash adds emphasis, variety, and informality to our writing. Although this mark can be used in place of commas, semicolons, colons, and parentheses, indiscriminate use will tend to reduce its impact. As a general rule, the em dash should not be used when another punctuation mark (eg, the comma or the colon) will suffice. So under what conditions should we use the em dash?

Use an em dash

◆ To indicate a sudden interruption or break in thought
◆ To set off and emphasize an appositive or a parenthetic expression
◆ To set off introductory elements from their explanations or before a word that sums up a preceding series
◆ To provide rhythmic and visual variety

To indicate a sudden interruption or break in thought

A dash can be used "to show an abrupt break in thought or to separate an afterthought from the main part of the sentence" (Sabin, p. 56). The following examples illustrate the use of the em dash to indicate a sudden interruption or break in thought:

> *The physician wanted the best for his patient—the most quantity and the best quality of life.*

The dash above is needed to separate the main clause from the phrase *the most quantity and the best quality of life.* This phrase expands on what the physician wanted but does not fit neatly into the construction of the independent clause to allow for other punctuation. Let's look at another example:

> *. . . , for in these small animals, drugs generally—not always, but generally—have much shorter half-lives than they do in larger animals.*

The phrase *not always, but generally* qualifies the main clause *drugs generally have much shorter half-lives than they do in larger animals* but consists of nonrestrictive information that certainly interrupts the thought of the sentence. The phrase almost sounds like an **aside**, and the dashes set it off properly from the main clause.

To set off and emphasize an appositive or a parenthetic expression

When we want to set off and emphasize nonrestrictive material, em dashes are the marks to use. We noted in Chapter 2 that nonrestrictive material is usually set off by commas. In Chapter 6, we will learn that parentheses may also be used to set off nonrestrictive material under certain conditions. For our purposes here, we need to know that <u>dashes emphasize</u> and <u>parentheses de-emphasize</u> the information they set apart.

In the following examples, the information set off by em dashes is nonrestrictive—the sentence makes sense without it:

> *Certain factors—sex, age, physical conditioning, and genetic predispositions—affect the seriousness of the reaction.*

The phrase *sex, age, physical conditioning, and genetic predispositions* is an appositive. Although the sentence makes sense without these specifics, the reader may wish to know what they are. A similar example follows:

> *The tools of managed care—credentialing, case management, utilization control, use of information systems, and efficiency—have been used to lower cost and improve quality.*

Consider what would result if we punctuated this sentence without the em dashes:

> *The tools of managed care, credentialing, case management, utilization control, use of information systems, and efficiency, have been used to lower cost and improve quality.*

We can see that the commas do <u>not</u> suffice to clarify the relationship between the general noun phrase *tools of managed care* and the specific serial appositive. Without dashes (or parentheses) to set off the appositive, the sentence is confusing.

Besides appositives, other types of nonrestrictive material can be set off by em dashes. In the next example, a parenthetic expression is set off by the em dashes:

> *The second main idea is that rate-controlled drug delivery extends the permissible intervals between doses—sometimes to an unprecedented degree—thus simplifying regimens.*

In this sentence, the author has emphasized his opinion by setting it off with a pair of em dashes.

To set off introductory elements from their explanation or before a word that sums up a preceding series

Each of the next two sentences begins with a series that is set off from summarizing or explanatory information presented later in the sentence:

> *The Japanese beetle, the starling, the gypsy moth—these pests all came from abroad.*

> *Sex, age, physical conditioning, and genetic predispositions—all of these factors affect the severity of the reaction.*

To provide rhythmic and visual variety

Judicious use of em dashes can add zest, variety, clarity, and even emotion to our writing. These dashes can accommodate variation in sentence structure. Consider the following examples, showing identical information but with variations in sentence structure and punctuation. Which of these two versions is clearer?

> *The principal risks of this surgery are infection, hemorrhage, shock, and poor healing of the incision, if the patient is cachectic.*

> *The principal risks of this surgery are infection, hemorrhage, shock, and—if the patient is cachectic—poor healing of the incision.*

The first version above is ambiguous; the reader cannot be certain whether all these risks or only *poor healing of the incision* pertains to the cachectic patient. By rearranging the sentence structure and using em dashes to set off *if the patient is cachectic*, we clarify the relationships among these elements, thereby showing that being cachectic places a patient at risk specifically for poor healing of the incision.

Now consider the following sentences that are identical except for their punctuation. Which do you think is more effective? Why?

The groups battled ferociously for tort reform, just as ferociously as they battle for our reputations when we find ourselves in a claim or lawsuit.

The groups battled ferociously for tort reform—just as ferociously as they battle for our reputations when we find ourselves in a claim or lawsuit.

Clearly, the content of this sentence is associated with strong feelings. Setting off the dependent clause by a dash emphasizes just how "ferociously" the groups battled. Furthermore, note the visual effectiveness of the dash as it breaks up the text.

THE EN DASH

Use an en dash

◆ To show a relational distinction in compound words
◆ As the minus symbol

The en dash is slightly longer than a **hyphen** and shorter than an em dash:

hyphen (-)
en dash (–)
em dash (—)

Let's look at the primary function of the en dash.

To show a relational distinction in compound words

The en dash "shows relational distinction in a hyphenated or compound modifier, one element of which consists of two words or a hyphenated word, or when the word being modified is a compound" (Iverson, p. 213). By clarifying relationships, this mark carries particular importance for the information we write and edit. Here are some examples:

Tay-Sachs–related disease
non–self-governing group
manic-depressive–like symptoms
healthcare–related problems OR health care–related problems

In each of these examples, the compound is either hyphenated (*Tay-Sachs, self-governing,* and *manic-depressive*) or understood to be a unit (*health care* or *healthcare*). The en dash clarifies the relationship between the word that it connects with the compound and the compound.

As the minus symbol

In mathematical formulas, the en dash may be used as the minus symbol.

OTHER USES OF DASHES

Several other uses of dashes deserve passing mention:

The em dash may be used before the name of the person to whom a quotation is attributed when that name is apart from the text.

> *I think, therefore I am.*
> —Rene Descartes

The two other dashes, the two-em dash and the three-em dash, serve limited but specific functions. Both of these dashes are set close to the preceding letter but are followed by a regular space before the line continues:

The two-em dash indicates missing letters in a name or other word.

> *Dr. T——examined the patient Ms. L——after taking her history.*

The three-em dash is used to show missing words. In the example below, the three-em dash indicates that the doctor's full name has been omitted.

> *The patient was referred to Dr.———for treatment.*

Because so many writers ignore the en dash and often use a hyphen in its place, some writers question its survival. Note that although AMA does not use the en dash between the extremes in ranges, CBE (pp. 54–55) and a number of other general style manuals do. The rules and prohibitions pertaining to the use of hyphens to express ranges (discussed in Chapter 7) are similar to those pertaining to the en dash (in those style manuals that endorse its use for this purpose).

1. **En dashes should be used for which of the following?**

   a. To set off introductory elements.
   b. To precede a name in an attribution.
   c. To provide rhythmic and visual variety.
   d. To show relational distinction in compound words.

2. **Table 6 illustrates the change in agency R&D budgets from 1979 to 2000.**

   What punctuation is needed in this sentence?

   a. No changes.
   b. An en dash between the two dates.
   c. An em dash between the two dates.
   d. Substitution of the preposition *to* with *through.*

3. **Which statement about em dashes is correct?**

   a. They should not be used in running text.
   b. They should show relational distinction in compound words.
   c. They should be used to set off and emphasize appositive or parenthetic expressions.
   d. They should be used between consecutive numbers only in lists and tables but not in running text.

4. **A minus symbol is shown by which of the following?**

   a. An en dash.
   b. An em dash.
   c. A two-em dash.
   d. A three-em dash.

5. **To ensure several patients' privacy, you decide to mention them by title (Ms., Mrs., Mr., Dr.) and by the first letter in their last names. To show that the remaining letters are missing, you would follow the capital letter with which of the following?**

   a. An en dash.
   b. An em dash.
   c. A two-em dash.
   d. A three-em dash.

6. **The responsible exercising of this power requires physicians to attend to the value of fairness, understood as each person's receiving his or her share of a valuable social resource held in common—medical care as a common good.**

   Which of the following is needed in this sentence?

   a. No changes.
   b. A comma between *common* and *medical.*
   c. An em dash to replace the comma after *fairness.*
   d. A pair of en dashes to replace the comma and the em dash.

7. **Additionally, divalent metal ions, calcium or magnesium or both are required to activate the complement pathways.**

   Which of the following is needed in this sentence?

   a. No changes.
   b. A comma between *both* and *are.*
   c. An en dash between *both* and *are.*
   d. A pair of em dashes, one in place of the comma after *ions* and the other before *are.*

The following items have blank spaces. Choose the punctuation mark that best fits in the blank space.

8. **Obesity, diabetes, coronary disease, and hypertension ___ these diseases demand the serious attention of the medical community and call for more aggressive patient education.**

   a. A colon.
   b. A comma.
   c. An em dash.
   d. A semicolon.

9. **The candidate has disturbing beliefs on health care reform ___ a crucial issue for the medical establishment and the country right now.**

   a. A colon.
   b. An en dash.
   c. An em dash.
   d. A semicolon.

10. A study of 30 black children from State X who had nutritional rickets found that all had been breastfed without receiving the supplemental vitamin and that more than half presented with the disease in the final 2 years of the 10-year observational period ____ a strong suggestion that incidence is on the rise.

  a. A comma.
  b. An en dash.
  c. An em dash.
  d. A semicolon.

11. The differential diagnosis included sickle cell ____ thalassemia disease.

  a. A comma.
  b. An en dash.
  c. An em dash.
  d. No punctuation.

Parentheses and Square Brackets ( ), [ ]

> **Parentheses <u>de-emphasize</u>.** Like nonrestrictive appositives, parenthetic material can be deleted without altering the sentence's meaning; parentheses are used <u>only</u> with nonrestrictive material.

We have learned that nonrestrictive material can be set off by commas and by em dashes. As a reminder, the examples below show how commas and em dashes may be used for this purpose:

This procedure, a standard therapy, is almost always effective.

Certain factors—sex, age, physical conditioning, and genetic predispositions—affect the seriousness of the reaction.

Parentheses offer a third alternative for handling such nonessential information. But whereas em dashes emphasize the nonrestrictive material they set off, parentheses do just the opposite. Another difference between parentheses and em dashes is that the dashes may set off both restrictive and nonrestrictive material, whereas parenthetic expressions are always nonrestrictive.

WHEN TO USE PARENTHESES

Use parentheses to set off nonrestrictive material when dashes would be too emphatic and commas might cause confusion. Parentheses may enclose explanatory words, phrases, or clauses when the intent is to de-emphasize their role in the sentence (sometimes parenthetic expressions may even consist of one or more sentences).

Use parentheses

- ◆ With supplementary information
- ◆ With abbreviations
- ◆ With parenthetic plurals
- ◆ With directions to the reader
- ◆ With enumerations
- ◆ With percentages
- ◆ With other punctuation marks

The following examples show various constructions that call for the use of parentheses.

With supplementary information

The internal skeleton is composed of the cricoid ring (which supports the arytenoid and corniculate cartilages) and the first tracheal ring.

The parentheses above set off the nonrestrictive relative clause *which supports the arytenoid and corniculate cartilages* that provides supplementary information about the cricoid ring.

The next sentence also encloses explanatory material in parentheses:

Discrepant EIA results (ie, reactive with a nonreactive repeat) were tested a third time for comparison.

In the next sentence, commas would be insufficient for avoiding confusion:

The tools of managed care (credentialing, case management, utilization control, uses of information systems, and efficiency) have been used to lower cost and improve quality.

If commas alone had been used, the explanatory series *credentialing, case management, utilization control, uses of information systems, and efficiency* would not be set off clearly from the subject of the sentence, *The tools of managed care.* Furthermore, the sentence becomes easier to read with the visual assistance that the parentheses provide.

If, however, we wanted to emphasize the specific tools of managed care, we would use a pair of em dashes, as shown in Chapter 5:

The tools of managed care—credentialing, case management, utilization control, uses of information systems, and efficiency—have been used to lower cost and improve quality.

Again, see how the em dashes set off the explanatory series—much more emphatically than do the parentheses in the first version of the sentence.

With abbreviations

We are all familiar with the convention of introducing an abbreviation within parentheses:

Problem-based learning (PBL) has been shown to be an effective educational method for the third-year surgery clerkship.

An abbreviation that will be used throughout the rest of a document (AMA style recommends abbreviating if the term appears at least 5 times) follows immediately after the expanded form and is enclosed in parentheses at first mention. Thereafter, the abbreviation is used in place of the expanded form. Note that the expanded form is presented in lowercase letters, unless the expansion contains a proper noun, is a formal name, or begins a sentence (Iverson, p. 276).

magnetic resonance imaging (MRI)
BUT *Centers for Disease Control (CDC)*

Sticklers [including such literary luminaries as AMWA's Edie Schwager] advise us not to begin a sentence with an abbreviation: "Avoid starting a sentence (footnotes are exceptions) with a number or an abbreviation, especially a Greek letter or other such symbol" (Schwager, p. 164). Instead, the expanded form is spelled out to start the sentence.

With parenthetic plurals

The next example contains parenthetic plurals. Note that when parenthetic plurals are used, the verb remains singular and the opening parenthesis is set next to the preceding word (as shown):

> *The name(s) of the patient(s) is confidential.*

With directions to the reader

Parentheses are used also to give directions to the reader. These may include various citations for tables, figures, references in a text, identification within a figure legend, and other forms of identification:

> *An appropriate curvilinear incision should be made near the middle of the wire (Figure 5).*

> *One of the authors (J.B.A.) had investigated the process earlier.*

With enumerations

To divide a short list of enumerated elements that are run in and indicated by numerals or lowercase italic letters, parentheses may be used to enclose the numerals or letters (Iverson, p. 216).

> *The room should be equipped with (1) a desk, (2) appropriate laboratory forms, (3) an examining table, and (4) two chairs.*

The authors of many manuscripts that cross my desk seem to suffer from a compulsion to number items in a series when such enumeration serves no purpose whatsoever. Often this practice only adds clutter to already complex text. Be sure a good reason (eg, ranked order) exists for inserting parenthetic numbers or letters. Compare the following, with and without parenthetic enumerators:

> *These objectives include determining the relationship between PvO_2 and the three factors (1) CI, (2) DO_2, and (3) UO_2; determining the relationship between systemic lactate accumulation and all these factors; and determining the relationship between VO_2 and DO_2 in control and endotoxic ponies.*

> *These objectives include determining the relationship between PvO_2 and the three factors CI, DO_2, and UO_2; determining the relationship between systemic lactate accumulation and all these factors; and determining the relationship between VO_2 and DO_2 in control and endotoxic ponies.*

Longer enumerations may appear more effectively as vertical lists, and unless the items are in ranked order or some other reason exists for the parenthetic numbers or letters, bullets may sometimes be used more effectively.

With percentages

Often a sentence will contain both a number and the percentage of the total that number represents. The preferred practice is to place the percentage in parentheses so as "to give primacy to the original data" (Iverson, p. 518):

Of the 8325 patients studied, 2764 (33%) exhibited symptoms of the disease.

With other punctuation marks

Several guidelines apply to the use of parentheses in relation to other punctuation marks in a sentence:

◆ Never use a punctuation mark before an opening (left) parenthesis except in enumerations: for example, *as follows: (1).*
◆ Any punctuation mark can follow a closing parenthesis.
◆ Only periods, question marks, and exclamation points may precede the closing parenthesis.

WHEN TO USE SQUARE BRACKETS

Use square brackets

◆ To insert editorial commentary or supplementary matter into quotations
◆ To enclose parenthetical expressions within parenthetical expressions

The British term "square brackets" distinguishes these from other kinds of punctuation marks. In other parts of the world, "bracket" can mean parentheses ("round brackets"), the brackets ({ }) often called "braces" or "curly brackets," or angle (< >) brackets (CBE, p. 58). Although used less often than parentheses, **square brackets** serve several specific functions. Examples of each follow:

To insert editorial commentary or supplementary matter into quotations

When an author inserts comments or supplementary information into quoted material, enclosing the inserted matter in brackets indicates to the reader that this information is not part of the original quotation.

"The peak of the epidemic occurred in the following year [1989]."

"The theoretical basis for this approach [not described in this report] is clear and unequivocal."

An author may also insert the bracketed Latin word *sic* (meaning "so" or "thus") to indicate an error or peculiarity in the spelling or grammar of the preceding word in an original quotation. Because this usage calls attention to errors in the quoted material, *sic* should be used judiciously. Ordinarily, the word *sic* is italicized, but the brackets surrounding it are not (Sabin, p. 82).

The author wrote, "In these cases, chemotherapy is more effective then [sic] *radiation."*

The writer has inserted the bracketed *sic* to indicate that the incorrect spelling of "than" is recognized but retained as part of the original sentence being quoted.

To enclose parenthetic expressions within parenthetic expressions

In scientific text, parenthetic constructions may occur consecutively under certain circumstances. In text, a parenthetic expression within a parenthetic expression is enclosed by square brackets:

The increase in fasting blood glucose levels was mildly greater in the study group than in the placebo group (16.2 mg/dL vs 1.8 mg/dL [0.90 vs 0.10 mmol/L], P = .04).

decreased serum alkaline phosphatase level (305 ± 48 U/L; P<.05 [Table 3])

In mathematical formulas, "parentheses are generally used for the innermost units, with parentheses changed to brackets when the formula is parenthetical" (Iverson, p 218):

$t = d(r_1 - r_2)$
BUT the equation suggested by this phenomenon ($t = d[r_1 - r_2]$) can be applied in a variety of circumstances.

$a + [(b + c)/d] + e$

The AMA style manual recommends changing "parentheses to brackets or brackets to parentheses in a formula as needed, working from inside out, starting with parentheses, to brackets, to braces" (Iverson, p. 218). This manual contains additional guidelines and sources for the use of parentheses and brackets in chemical and mathematical formulas.

Up to this point in the module, we have studied punctuation marks that mostly separate grammatical elements. In Chapter 7, we will discuss the mark that joins words that belong together: the hyphen.

1. **Which of the following has the best punctuation for the sentence?**

   a. Many dermatophytes that invade hair form compounds, thought to be pteridines, that fluoresce green when exposed to ultraviolet light, (Wood's light).
   b. Many dermatophytes that invade hair form compounds (thought to be pteridines) that fluoresce green when exposed to ultraviolet light, Wood's light.
   c. Many dermatophytes that invade hair form compounds (thought to be pteridines), that fluoresce green when exposed to ultraviolet light (Wood's light).
   d. Many dermatophytes that invade hair form compounds (thought to be pteridines) that fluoresce green when exposed to ultraviolet light (Wood's light).

2. **Which of the following has the best punctuation for the sentence?**

   a. In all, 85% (7420) of eligible students in grades 6 through 8 and 80.5% (7221) of eligible students in grades 9 through 12 were surveyed.
   b. In all, 85% (7420) of eligible students in grades 6 through 8, and 80.5% (7221) of eligible students in grades 9 through 12 were surveyed.
   c. In all, 7420 (85%) of eligible students in grades 6 through 8 and 7221 (80.5%) of eligible students in grades 9 through 12 were surveyed.
   d. In all, 7,420 (85%) of eligible students in grades 6 through 8 and 7,221 (80.5%) of eligible students in grades 9 through 12 were surveyed.

3. **Generally, anthropophilic fungi, (*M audouini, T mentagrophytes var. interdigitale, T rubrum, T tonsurans,* and *E floccosum*) cause chronic diseases that evoke little tissue reaction.**

   Which of the following best describes punctuation in this sentence?

   a. No changes are needed.
   b. The comma after *fungi* should be deleted.
   c. A comma should be inserted after the closing parenthesis.
   d. The parenthetic information should be set off by a pair of em dashes.

4. **A number of medical professional organizations (the American Medical Association, the American Academy of Pediatrics, and others) have advocated also for more environmental health training.**

In this sentence, you are introducing the names of these associations in an article and will be mentioning them many times again, so you want to abbreviate them. How will you do this?

  a. Replace the full names with the abbreviations.
  b. Remove the parentheses so that you can insert the abbreviations in parentheses.
  c. Retain the current parentheses and insert the proper abbreviation in square brackets after each association's name.
  d. Change the current parentheses to square brackets and insert the proper abbreviation in parentheses after each association name.

5. **"I think if the FNB [Food and Nutrition Board] were to reconvene, there would be a strong push to establish 32 ng/mL (80 nmol/L) as the lower end of normal."**

Which of the following accurately describes the punctuation in this quotation?

  a. Square brackets properly enclose *Food and Nutrition Board*.
  b. Parentheses, not square brackets, should enclose *Food and Nutrition Board*.
  c. The alternate expression *80 nmol/L* should be enclosed in square brackets.
  d. The abbreviation *FNB* and the spelled out name of the board should be reversed and the abbreviation enclosed within parentheses.

6. **Texas, like the rest of the country, has made progress protecting its workforce from the hazards of secondhand smoke, (Table 1.)**

What punctuation changes are needed in this sentence?

  a. None.
  b. The word *workforce* should be hyphenated.
  c. The word *its* is a possessive and needs an apostrophe.
  d. The comma after *smoke* should be deleted, and the period after Table 1 should be moved to follow the closing parenthesis.

The Hyphen (-)

If you take hyphens seriously, you will surely go mad.
—John Benbow

These less-than-heartening words from an old Oxford University Press style guide have never been more true. As our language evolves and technology explodes, new ideas, new words, new combinations of words, and new expressions develop—relentlessly! And hyphens are often caught up in this bewildering torrent of change. To wit, the section on hyphens accounts for the greatest proportion of punctuation changes in the newest revision (the 10th edition) of the *AMA Manual of Style.* Much of the material in this chapter is taken from the AMA and the Chicago style manuals.

When I was young, we spoke of *medical care.* Sometime during the last 15 or 20 years, medical care became *health care* or *health-care,* which often appears now as the solidified compound *healthcare.* The 10th edition of the AMA manual has retained the two-word, unhyphenated compound *health care*—at least for the time being (C. Iverson, written communication, February 2006). Other examples of new terms that were formerly hyphenated are *database, website,* and *online.* Within this rather messy context, let's see if we can make some sense out of hyphenation.

So far in this workshop, we have been looking mostly at sentence punctuation, defining relationships between and among phrases and clauses. Hyphens define relationships between words, joining them into single units. The tough question is whether or not to hyphenate. This question is not always answered easily. A few broad guidelines will help:

- ◆ First, consult the dictionary.
- ◆ Next, consult your style manual(s).
- ◆ If these sources do not help, ask whether confusion could possibly result if no hyphen were used to clarify relationships. If the words do not appear in the sources above, either hyphenated or solid, you must decide either to hyphenate, to solidify, or to leave the compound as unhyphenated two words.
- ◆ Consider the reader's ease in comprehending.
- ◆ Whatever you decide, be consistent!

Orthographic hyphens (those that are part of the spelling of the word) are always used (eg, *merry-go-round, hard-and-fast, great-grandfather*) and are found in the dictionary. **Temporary hyphens** (those needed to prevent ambiguity) are the ones that give us the most trouble. Fortunately, we do have some logical rules to keep us sane.

WHEN TO USE A HYPHEN

Use a hyphen

- To join two words used as a single unit <u>before</u> the noun they modify
- To join compound adjectival phrases, adverb-participle compounds, and adjective-noun compounds that have become commonplace
- To join words with certain prefixes and suffixes
- To aid the reader when words are not commonly found as a unit or when the meaning would otherwise be unclear

---

To join two words used as a single unit <u>before</u> the noun they modify

Temporary hyphens are used to form a single unit that serves as an adjective preceding a noun. When the same words follow the noun, they are usually not hyphenated. The following examples illustrate this difference:

short-acting benzodiazepines
BUT *the benzodiazepines are short acting*
[adverb + participle]

physician-patient relationship
BUT NOT *physician/patient relationship*
[2 nouns used coordinately as a modifier; see Chapter 8 for rules pertaining to the slash]

Osler-Weber-Rendu disease
BUT *the disease described by Osler, Weber, and Rendu*
[2 or more nouns used coordinately]

dose-related response
BUT *the response is dose related*
[noun + participle]

clearly related assumption
[adverb + participle; hyphens are not used after adverbs ending in -ly]

6-month-old infant
BUT *an infant 6 months old [or infant aged 6 months]*
[number + noun + adjective]

10- and 15-week intervals **BUT** *intervals of 10 and 15 weeks*
[number + noun with common base]

Note that in the next example, AMA (p. 209) chooses <u>not</u> to use a stand-alone prefix with a hyphen before a contrasting unhyphenated prefix.

hyperthyroid and hypothyroid girls
NOT *hyper- and hypothyroid girls*
[contrasting prefixes]

To join compound adjectival phrases, adverb-participle compounds, and adjective-noun compounds that have become commonplace

Certain familiar compounds are <u>hyphenated whether they precede or follow the noun they modify</u> (Iverson, p. 207). Note that *The Chicago Manual of Style*'s discussion of hyphens (pp. 299–308) also contains an extremely helpful section on how to punctuate compounds with various prefixes and suffixes, qualifying that the manual "illustrates not hard-and-fast rules but general patterns" (p. 302). Not all of the Chicago guidelines correspond to those of AMA style.

The following are a few examples of such commonplace expressions that are hyphenated before and after the noun.

mind-boggling suggestion
AND *his suggestion was mind-boggling*
[noun + participle]

matter-of-fact affect
AND *her affect was matter-of-fact*
[noun + adjectival prepositional phrase]

state-of-the-art equipment
AND *the equipment was state-of-the-art*
[noun + adjectival prepositional phrase]

short-term therapy
AND *the therapy was short-term*
[adjective + noun]

life-style considerations
AND *considerations of life-style*
[noun + noun]

Although a colon is used between the elements of ratios when they are expressed as numbers or abbreviations, ratios expressed as words use the word *to* instead of the colon, according to C. Iverson (written communication, February 2006).

the HbA_1:HbA_2 ratio
BUT *the ratio of HbA_1 **to** HbA_2*
*the ratio of smokers **to** nonsmokers*

Commonplace compounds like *the cost-benefit ratio* may appear hyphenated in some dictionaries but not in others. Deciding how to handle these compound expressions often requires judgment calls on our part. My best advice is to check your sources (including published articles), make your decision (keeping the reader's comprehension in mind), and then be consistent in your usage.

To join words with certain prefixes and suffixes

Compounds formed with most prefixes are usually solid words (eg, *automatic, paralegal,* and *extrasensory*). Other than the exceptions shown below, the following prefixes form solid, unhyphenated compounds: *ante-, anti-, bi-, co-, contra-, counter-, de-, extra-, infra-, inter-, micro-, mid-, neo-, non-, over-, pre-, post-, pro-, pseudo-, re-, semi-, sub-, super-, supra-, trans-, tri-, ultra-, un-,* and *under-* (Iverson, p. 211).

Similarly, certain suffixes combine into solid compounds (eg, *tooth**ache**, air**borne**, six**fold*** (BUT *6-**fold***), *wave**like***, and *state**wide***).

Hyphenate when the compound formed with the prefix or suffix forms an awkward combination of letters, such as two of the same vowel or three of the same consonant (eg, *intra-abdominal, bell-like, semi-independent*).

Exceptions:

Hyphenate a compound when the prefix precedes any of the following (Chicago, p. 307; Iverson, p. 211):

> a proper noun (*non-Latin*)
> a numeral (*pre-2000*)
> an abbreviation (*pre-HMO era*)

Use an en dash after a prefix combined with a compound term, whether hyphenated or consisting of two or more words (*non–self-sufficient, post–World War II*).

Certain words with repetitive letters (eg, *microorganism* and *cooperation*) are not hyphenated. Let your dictionary be your guide.

Hyphenate when the compound creates another meaning (*recreation* versus *re-creation, retreat* versus *re-treat*).

Certain other prefixes (*all-, self-,* and *ex-*) and suffixes (*-type, -elect,* and *-designate*) are used with hyphens in compounds whether they precede or follow the noun:

> *self-administered medications*
> **AND** *medications were self-administered*
>
> *president-elect*
> **BUT** *surgery chairman designate* [no hyphen with compound office]

Other examples of these prefixes and suffixes include *ex-chairman, all-student forum, end-stage renal disease,* and *Hodgkin-type lymphoma.*

To aid the reader when words are not commonly found as a unit or when the meaning would otherwise be unclear

Other hyphenated compounds are formed when words are not commonly found as a unit, when meaning would otherwise be unclear or ambiguous, or when two or more adjectives are used coordinately or as conflicting terms. The following are examples of words that are hyphenated regardless of their placement in the sentence because they belong together for the sake of clarity:

40 pack-years of smoking, light-years, half-time, double-blind, false-negative, and *false-positive*

In the next example, the hyphenated compound carries a different connotation than the more literal *cutting edge* that modifies the knife.

cutting-edge science
BUT *The knife's cutting edge was dull*
OR *The cutting edge of the knife was dull*

The next example (Iverson, p. 210) shows hyphenation to prevent ambiguity:

a small-bowel constriction (constriction of the small bowel)
a small bowel constriction (a small constriction of the bowel)

In the past, AMA has hyphenated fractions only when they are used as adjectives (eg, *his glass was one-half full* **BUT** *one half of the glass was empty*). In the 10th edition of the style manual, fractions will be hyphenated both as nouns and as adjectives, according to C. Iverson (written communication, February 2006).

Both the AMA and the Chicago style manuals contain many helpful examples to follow in making decisions about hyphenation. Don't forget to consult your dictionaries and your style manuals; above all, be consistent with whatever choice you make.

WHEN NOT TO USE A HYPHEN

Do **not** use a hyphen

- ◆ With most ranges in text
- ◆ With combinations of words commonly read as a unit
- ◆ After adverbs ending in *-ly*
- ◆ In Latin or non-English expressions used adjectivally
- ◆ In modifiers in which a letter or number is the second element

---

With most ranges in text

In running text, do <u>not</u> use hyphens to express ranges (Iverson, pp. 210–211). In text, a range must be expressed verbally. Can you explain why treatment of the range in the following sentence might cause confusion?

The study was conducted from 1990-1995.

Punctuated with the hyphen, the range in this sentence is ambiguous; we cannot tell whether the study ran for 5 years (from 1990 **to** 1995) or whether the range was inclusive and the study ran for 6 years (from 1990 **through** 1995). The AMA and CBE style manuals both advise expressing ranges in running text by using the preposition "to" or "through"—whichever applies—to clarify whether a range is exclusive.

estimated to range from 5% to 22%
NOT *from 5 to 22%* **OR** *from 5%-22%*

duration of illness ranged from 3 to 5 months **NOT** *from 3-5 months*

subjects aged from 20 through 35 years **NOT** *from 20-35 years*

Two exceptions to this rule not to hyphenate ranges in text may be made. Once the exact length of the range has been established clearly in a document, a hyphen may be used in text under the following conditions:

◆ When the ranges express fiscal years, academic years, life spans, or a study span
◆ When the ranges are presented within parentheses

The test was given during the 1999-2000 school year.

The findings were more conclusive in the 2000-2003 study.

The mean time from baseline examination (1995-1997) to diagnosis was 4.7 years (range, 2.4-7.4 years).

In tables and figures, hyphens may be used within ranges.

With combinations of words commonly read as a unit

As combinations of words become commonly read as a unit, the hyphen is no longer needed to ensure clarity. These combinations include many familiar expressions, compound names of diseases used as modifiers, and proper adjectives derived from geographic entities when used as noun or adjective formations (Iverson, p. 212).

health care services   primary care physician   African American student

squamous cell carcinoma   infectious disease specialist

pulmonary acid aspiration syndrome   sickle cell anemia

T cell [as a noun] **BUT** *T-cell marker*

After adverbs ending in *-ly*

You may have learned in grammar school that a hyphen does not follow adverbs ending in *-ly*. The rule still applies!

firmly held belief   frequently used procedure   strongly indicated approach

In Latin or non-English expressions used adjectivally

Foreign expressions and non–English-language phrases used as modifiers are not hyphenated. Most are treated as separate words and some are solidified (Iverson, p. 212).

> *ex post facto arrangement   ad nauseum repetition   antepartum condition*

Non-English words or expressions that have not made their way into standard English usage and do not appear in dictionaries should be italicized; more common expressions such as those shown above are not ordinarily italicized (Iverson, p. 271).

In modifiers in which a letter or number is the second element

The AMA manual (p. 212) does not hyphenate modifiers in which the second element consists of a letter or a number:

> *type 1 diabetes   grade A eggs   study 2 protocol*

The AMA manual uses numerals to express numbers most of the time; however, numbers that begin a sentence should be spelled out. In text, spelled-out numerals above 99 (ie, *one hundred, two hundred*) are not hyphenated, but those from 21 through 99 are (Iverson, pp. 511–513).

I never promised you that hyphens would be fun (while writing this module, I found *life span, life-span,* and *lifespan* among one online and two printed dictionaries). Many more rules, exceptions, and specifics regarding hyphenation exist, but I suspect that this chapter has given you enough to chew on for now. Each of you will encounter different hyphenation dilemmas in the course of your writing and editing, so different rules may apply to the specific terminology with which you are dealing. With the guidelines presented here as your foundation, you should be ready to attack your dictionaries and style manuals with a better understanding of whether or not to hyphenate.

1. **Activated dendritic cells then activate tumor specific CD8 T lymphocytes.**

   What punctuation does this sentence need?

   a. No changes.
   b. A hyphen between *tumor* and *specific*.
   c. A hyphen between *T* and *lymphocytes*.

2. **RBCs with demonstrated viability can be stored at 4°C for intervals well in excess of their 120-day in vivo life span.**

   What punctuation does this sentence need?

   a. No changes.
   b. A hyphen between *in* and *vivo*.
   c. No hyphen between *120* and *day*.

3. **Next, <u>B cell depleted</u> fraction was labeled with biotin-conjugated CD1c monoclonal antibodies and subsequently with antibiotin microbeads.**

   Which is the best punctuation for the underlined phrase?

   a. B cell depleted.
   b. B-cell depleted.
   c. B-cell-depleted.
   d. B-cell–depleted.

4. **A <u>10 to 20 mL sample</u> is drawn at least 24 hours after collection to avoid false-negative results.**

   Which is the best punctuation for the underlined phrase?

   a. 10-to-20 mL sample.
   b. 10-to-20-mL sample.
   c. 10- to 20 mL sample.
   d. 10- to 20-mL sample.

Which answer best follows AMA style in each of the following questions?

5. a. Next, patient/doctor communication was discussed.
   b. Next, patient-doctor communication was discussed.
   c. Next, patient–doctor communication was discussed.

6. a. The patient was calcium deficient.
   b. The patient was calcium-deficient.

7. a. 176 patients constituted the sample.
   b. One-hundred seventy-six patients constituted the sample.
   c. One-hundred seventy-six patients constituted the sample.
   d. One hundred seventy-six patients constituted the sample.

8. a. The surgeon feared that intracranial hemorrhage had occurred.
   b. The surgeon feared that intra-cranial hemorrhage had occurred.
   c. The surgeon feared that intra cranial hemorrhage had occurred.

9. a. The condition was first reported during the postHolocaust years.
   b. The condition was first reported during the post-Holocaust years.
   c. The condition was first reported during the post Holocaust years.

10. a. The campaign to immunize all preschool children was citywide.
    b. The campaign to immunize all preschool children was city wide.
    c. The campaign to immunize all preschool children was city-wide.

11. a. Table 1 shows age and sex adjusted relative-prevalence ratios for these associations between use of both types of corticosteroids and the presence of cataracts.
    b. Table 1 shows age- and sex-adjusted relative-prevalence ratios for the associations between the use of both types of corticosteroids and the presence of cataracts.
    c. Table 1 shows age-adjusted and sex-adjusted relative-prevalence ratios for the associations between the use of both types of corticosteroids and the presence of cataracts.

The Apostrophe and the Forward Slash (' /)

THE APOSTROPHE

The poor little **apostrophe** suffers rampant misuse. This mark has three completely independent uses, each of which applies under some circumstances but not others. Furthermore, because style manuals often differ on the rules, consistent use of a designated style is mandatory. Let's look at these three functions of the apostrophe.

Use an apostrophe

◆ To show possession or association
◆ To mark the omission of something in a contraction
◆ To form some plurals

To show possession or association

Possession can be indicated in two ways: the first is by means of a prepositional phrase. No apostrophe is used when a prepositional phrase expresses possession:

the characteristic signs of the disease

If we want to eliminate the prepositional phrase, we resort to the second form of expression, the possessive case: the case taken by a noun or pronoun when it is used to show possession or ownership. The apostrophe is used with the possessive case in nouns but not in pronouns:

the disease's characteristic signs

BUT *its characteristic signs*

Use of the apostrophe varies, however, depending upon the nature of the "possessing" noun or pronoun. Because "feelings [on this matter] sometimes run high," *The Chicago Manual of Style* advises its users to "modify or add to the exceptions" as they may wish (p. 281). The following rules and examples for the use of the apostrophe with the possessive case are mostly consistent with those in the AMA style manual (pp. 221–223).

RULE: For most <u>singular</u> common and proper nouns, form the possessive by adding <u>an apostrophe and the letter *s*</u>.

the surgeon's schedule	*the hospital's rules*	*Dr. Charles's patient*
a year's contract	*medicine's effect*	*Mr. Jones's problem*

Some proper nouns that are ordinarily excepted are *Moses'* law and *Jesus'* name. Check whatever style manual you are using to find such exceptions.

In the biomedical literature, another exception to this rule is gaining acceptance. **Eponyms** are "phrases or names derived from or including the name of a person or place" (Iverson, p. 469). For many years, eponyms have been used to describe diseases, syndromes, procedures, and tests by the names of the researchers who discovered or developed them: eg, *Moh's surgery, Crohn's disease, Alzheimer's disease, Fanconi's syndrome, Gilles de la Tourette's syndrome*, and *Gram's stain*. The possessive form has not been used, however, for eponyms named for patients or places (eg, *Lyme disease*), and when more than one researcher's name is carried in the descriptive term, the possessive apostrophe is never used (eg, *Creutzfelt-Jacob disease*). Medical dictionaries and style manuals have been somewhat inconsistent in abolishing this possessive usage, but others have quite definitely dropped the possessive form (eg, the edition of *Stedman's Medical Dictionary* published in 2000 shows *Gram stain* without the apostrophe). The CBE manual recommends eliminating altogether the possessive form of eponymous terms so that they can be distinguished from true possessives (CBE, p. 97). The AMA and CBE style manuals both contain interesting discussions that shed light on the evolution of this usage, but the trend is clearly moving in the direction of nonpossessive use, with no apostrophe (eg, *Down syndrome*).

RULE: For <u>plural</u> nouns (except for a few irregular plurals), form the possessive by adding <u>an apostrophe only</u>.

2 years' experience	*nurses' responsibilities*	*patients' noncompliance*

the Joneses' appointment [for more than 1 member of the Jones family]

RULE: For names of <u>organizations and associations</u>, if the organization's official name does not use the apostrophe, omit it.

Veterans Administration	*American Medical Writers Association*

RULE: For <u>joint possession</u>, use an apostrophe and the letter *s* <u>only after the last noun</u> in the series; for <u>separate possession</u>, <u>both nouns</u> take the possessive case.

Strunk and White's little book

BUT *Strunk's and White's careers*

Occasionally, following the rules produces such an awkward plural possessive that rephrasing with a preposition becomes a more graceful alternative. For example, in the singular, *attorney-general's case* is fine, but if more than one attorney general is involved in a discovery, *attorneys-general's discovery* should probably be changed into the prepositional phrase *discovery of the attorneys general.*

RULE: For <u>possessive pronouns</u>, do <u>not</u> use an apostrophe or the letter *s*.

Possessive pronouns (*my, mine, your, yours, his, hers, its, ours, your, yours, their, theirs,* and *whose*) are born possessive; that is, they are inherently possessive and need no punctuation to indicate their possessiveness. The possessive pronoun used may vary depending on whether it immediately precedes the noun it modifies (*That is **my** choice*) or stands apart from its noun (*The choice is **mine***). Do not confuse possessive pronouns with contractions (Sabin, pp. 287–288).

To mark the omission of something in a contraction

A **contraction** is "a shortened form of a word or phrase in which an apostrophe indicates the omitted letters or words" (Sabin, p. 638). We can easily avoid confusing possessive pronouns with contractions by identifying what contractions actually mean and recognizing that the apostrophe in them represents something that has been omitted.

Possessive pronoun	*Contraction*
your	*you're (you are)*
its	*it's (it is)*
their	*they're (they are)*
whose	*who's (who is)*

To form some plurals

Use an apostrophe and the letter *s* to form the plural of letters, signs, symbols, numbers, and abbreviations when adding an *s* alone would cause confusion. Do <u>not</u> use an apostrophe to form the plural of an all-capital abbreviation or of numerals (Iverson, p. 222). The following examples show when the apostrophe is needed and when it is not:

*plot the **x**'s and **y**'s*   *mind your **p**'s and **q**'s*   *her **l**'s look like **1**'s*

BUT   *EEGs   RBCs   IQs   woman in her 40s   the late 1990s* **BUT** *the '90s*

When in doubt, let clarity and your style manual be your guide for the use of apostrophes.

THE FORWARD SLASH

The forward **slash** (known also as the **virgule**, the oblique bar, the diagonal, and the slant line) is used mainly in mathematical expressions to symbolize *divided by* or *per*. For text, the CBE style manual calls this mark "a lazy substitute for the comma or hyphen or full expression" and recommends usually punctuating a series with commas and punctuating coordinate modifiers with hyphens or en dashes. The CBE manual advises that in scientific writing, the slash "should be reserved for mathematical expressions and its few other specialized uses," which include the symbol for division (eg, *3/4*), expressions of rate or concentration (*30 mol/L*), and several others (pp. 64–65). <u>The forward slash should be used rarely in text.</u>

For our purposes, the main functions of the forward slash are the following:

Use the forward slash

◆ As *per* in units of measure when at least one element is a numeric quantity and the other is a number or unit of measure

◆ As *and* and *or,* **BUT** writing out the full expression is usually clearer

◆ To divide material (in equations and dates)

As *per* in units of measure when at least one element is a numeric quantity and the other is a number or unit of measure

The following examples show how and when the forward slash should be used in text:

a 10- to 20-min/mile pace
OR *a pace of 10 to 20 min/mile* [both forms contain a numeric quantity and a unit of measure]

The hemoglobin level was 7.8 g/dL

BUT *60 beats per minute* [because beats is not a unit of measure, the slash would be incorrect]

a potassium concentration of 4.5 mmol/L
BUT NOT *4.5 mmol of potassium/L* [because the slash is not used in a *per* construction when a prepositional phrase intervenes between the two elements]

The results are expressed in milliliters per minute [the slash is not used when neither element contains a specific numerical quantity]

2 days per year [the slash is not used in nontechnical expressions]

As *and* and *or,* BUT writing out the full expression is usually clearer

The slash is viewed somewhat more tolerantly by AMA style than by CBE style. The AMA manual states, "When 2 terms are of equal weight in an expression and [the word] *and* is meant between them to express this, [the slash] can be retained to show this" (Iverson, p. 212).

MD/PhD student   Jekyll/Hyde personality   prenatal/obstetrics settings

Nevertheless, this style manual also warns that if "any likelihood of ambiguity" exists, the sentence should be reworded. The *he/she* construction should be avoided for the most part, either by substituting the word *or* for the slash (*he or she*) or by rephrasing into the plural to neutralize the gender (*they*).

The AMA style manual advises also changing the slash "when 2 separate individuals are implied in a relationship," distinguishing between the *physician-patient relationship* (when the relationship is between physician and patient) and *the physician/patient* duality when the physician <u>is</u> the patient (Iverson, p. 214).

As always, clarity is the overriding goal. Consider the following:

Treatment includes surgery plus radiation/chemotherapy.

Treatment includes surgery plus radiation or chemotherapy or both.

See how replacing the slash with an explicit spelling out of the possible therapies eliminates any possible confusion by stating clearly that, in addition to surgery, the patient may undergo radiation alone, chemotherapy alone, or radiation and chemotherapy together. <u>Avoid using the *and/or* construction</u>, which is not only lazy but also imprecise.

To divide material (in equations and dates)

In fractions and equations that are run into the text, use the slash to separate numerator and denominator: eg, $y = (r_1 + r_2) / (p_1 + p_2)$ (Iverson, p. 215; Chicago, p. 541).

For dates, *5/11/99* may be used only in tables and figures; **BUT** in text, use *May 23, 1999*. Avoiding the slash construction in text is particularly important for international publications, in which the date starts with the day rather than the month (*23 May 1999*).

For ratios that consist of numbers or abbreviations, AMA style prefers using a colon rather than a slash; for ratios involving words, use the word "to" (C. Iverson, written communication, February 2006):

the SUN:Cr ratio was greater than 10:1
BUT *the serum urea nitrogen **to** creatinine ratio was greater than 10:1.*

Quotations will be the topic of the next chapter. In it, we will learn how to use quotation marks and ellipses correctly. The restrictions on the use of ellipses may surprise you.

1. **Which of the following refers to a single year?**

    a. We hope to avoid the recent year's vaccine shortage.
    b. We hope to avoid the recent years' vaccine shortage.

2. **Which of the following is correct?**

    a. The newly formed institute published its mission statement.
    b. The newly formed institute published it's mission statement.

3. **Which of the following expressions best describes the results for a patient who underwent more than one MRI?**

    a. The MRI's results suggested metastatic carcinoma.
    b. The MRIs' results suggested metastatic carcinoma.
    c. The MRIs's results suggested metastatic carcinoma.

4. **Which form below is preferred in current usage?**

    a. Gram stain.
    b. Gram's stain.
    c. Grams' stain.
    d. Grams's stain.

5. **Which of the following expressions uses the apostrophe correctly for joint possession?**

    a. Banting and Best's pioneering research in diabetes was cited.
    b. Banting's and Best's pioneering research in diabetes was cited.

6. **Which of the following expressions uses the apostrophe correctly?**

    a. The protocol called for a 3 month's trial of the experimental drug.
    b. The protocol called for a 3 months' trial of the experimental drug.

7. **Which of the following expressions uses the apostrophe correctly?**

    a. The mens and women's test scores were compared.
    b. The men's and women's test scores were compared.
    c. The mens' and womens' test scores were compared.

8. Which of the following expressions is preferred in text?

   a. 7/24/07.
   b. July 24, 2007.
   c. Either expression is equally acceptable.

9. Which of the following expressions would be incorrect in running text?

   a. The patient was given 1200 IU of calcium/d.
   b. The patient was given 1200 IU of calcium per day.
   c. The patient was given 1200 IU/d of calcium.

10. Which of the following is preferred?

   a. Several organizations have recommended initiating screening earlier and/or more frequently for patients whose family histories suggest that they are at moderately increased risk of developing cancer.
   b. Several organizations have recommended initiating screening earlier, more frequently, or both for patients whose family histories suggest that they are at moderately increased risk of developing cancer.

Quotation Marks and Ellipses (" " . . .)

Quotations may be direct or indirect. A **direct quotation** consists of the exact words taken directly from another source, whereas an **indirect quotation** restates or rephrases that source's exact words and may be introduced by words like *whether, when,* or *that*:

> **Direct:** *The patient asked, "When will I be discharged from the hospital?"*
> **Indirect:** *The patient asked when she would be discharged from the hospital.*

Direct quotations may consist of dialogue or material that has been written or published. In this chapter, we will review the rules for the uses of double and single quotation marks and discuss their use in relation to other punctuation. Also, we'll learn how to show that some material within a quotation has been omitted.

USES OF QUOTATION MARKS

Use quotation marks

- ◆ To indicate material taken directly from another person or writer
- ◆ To give special emphasis to selected words or phrases
- ◆ To indicate titles of certain parts of complete published works

---

Given these three main functions of quotation marks, let's now look more specifically at each one.

To indicate material taken directly from another person or writer

Direct quotations may be handled in one of two styles: the quotations may be run in to the text, or they may be set off from the text in a block. The length of the quotation determines which of these forms is appropriate. Note that for conversational dialogue, the length of the quotation that may be set in run-on style has no limit (Iverson, p. 218).

RULE: Use quotation marks to enclose a direct quotation of no more than 4 typewritten lines.

The following example of a direct quotation that is run in uses double quotation marks around the quoted material:

> *Irby, in delineating legal guidelines for dismissing medical students, has underscored this reluctance on the part of faculty to point out problems: "Only in extreme cases," he says, "have faculty been willing to make negative evaluations."*

The next example shows how a block quotation would be handled. The quotation is indented, and no quotation marks are used.

Regarding the choice of styles for quotations, *The Chicago Manual of Style* (p. 447) states the following about block quotations:

> Block quotations are not enclosed in quotation marks and always start a new line. They may be indented or set in smaller type or a different font from the text; they may have unjustified right-hand margins or less space between lines. These matters are normally decided by the publisher's designer or by journal style. Authors preparing block quotations should avoid such devices (unless otherwise advised by their publishers) and simply use the indention feature of their word processors.

If a block quotation contains another quotation, set off the embedded quote with double quotation marks (Iverson, p. 221).

When the quoted material is run in and consists of two or more paragraphs from a single source, place opening quotation marks before the beginning of each paragraph but closing quotation marks only after the final paragraph (Sabin, p. 77). If the paragraphs consist of dialogue, place the remarks of each speaker within opening and closing double quotation marks.

> *"Have the laboratory studies been reported yet?"*
> *"Yes, doctor."*
> *"Well, why aren't they in the chart?"*

RULE: Use single quotation marks to set off quotations <u>within</u> quotations.

> *The professor asked, "Have you referred to the article 'Uses of Marijuana'?"*

The tricky part of dealing with quotation marks is placing the other punctuation that is involved with the quoted material. The rule below is consistent with American English (and AMA) style.

RULE: Place periods and commas inside quotation marks; colons and semicolons, outside. Question marks and exclamation points go inside only if they are part of the quotation itself.

> *How should we deal with the issue of the "right to die"?*
> *The coach said, "Go for the gold!"*
> *Calling the speaker "out of order," the chairman left.*

Note that CBE style does not follow the American style for punctuating quotations, advocating instead the British style, which is similar to that used in Canada and other countries influenced by the United Kingdom. British style calls for primary use of single quotation marks with secondary use of double quotation marks to set off quotations within quotations. Both British and CBE style place the closing quotation marks <u>before</u> the closing punctuation mark of the sentence that contains the quotation. British style places "only those punctuation points that appeared in the original material . . . within the quotation marks; all others follow the closing quotation marks" (Chicago, p. 243). Some of these differences are shown below:

American:	*How should we deal with the issue of the "right to die"?*
British:	*How should we deal with the issue of the 'right to die'?*
American:	*The coach said, "Go for the gold!"*
British:	*The coach said, 'Go for the gold!'*
American:	*Calling the speaker "out of order," the chairman left.*
British:	*Calling the speaker 'out of order', the chairman left.*

Finally, quoted material does not always need to be set off by a comma. In the sentence below, the quotation serves as the subject, which should never be separated from its verb by a comma:

> *"Why is the patient still bleeding?" was the surgeon's question.*

To give special emphasis to selected words or phrases

Quotation marks may be used to enclose "coined words, slang, nicknames, and words or phrases used ironically or facetiously" the first time they are mentioned (Iverson, p. 220). Quotation marks may also be used for words used in an unusual way and for deliberate misspelling or grammatical deviation. Like most punctuation devices that emphasize selected material, quotation marks when used for this purpose should not be overworked; used excessively, this practice may become "cutesy." A word or phrase that follows the expression *so-called* should <u>not</u> be enclosed in quotation marks:

> *Erhlich's "magic bullet"*
> **BUT** *Erlich's so-called magic bullet*

> *Used cars are now marketed as "preowned" cars.*

Other material that should <u>not</u> ordinarily be enclosed in quotation marks includes terms being defined, non-English expressions, or words to be emphasized; in these cases, italics are preferred. Occasionally, quotation marks are necessary to clarify that an expression is being used in a special or unusual manner. The AMA style manual (p. 220) gives the following example:

> *In many publications, "running feet" on left-hand pages face the "gutter" at the bottom of the page.*

To indicate titles of certain parts of complete published works

In text—but not in bibliographic format—certain titles are enclosed in quotation marks. Generally, quotation marks enclose parts (eg, chapters and journal articles) of complete published works; also, these marks enclose the titles of other short works such as poems, pamphlets and brochures, essays, lectures, presented papers, dissertations, theses, and parts of the same article (eg, "Methods" section). Titles of books and journals are expressed in italics, not in quotation marks.

USES OF ELLIPSES

Use ellipses

◆ To indicate an omission from quoted material
◆ In tables to indicate that no data were available

Leave spaces between the points that make up an ellipsis.
At the end of a sentence, an ellipsis takes a final period.

To indicate an omission from quoted material

Although **ellipses** have metastasized ever since the first electric typewriter allowed the typist to press the period key to achieve infinite repetition, these punctuation marks have <u>only</u> one legitimate function in text: to indicate the omission of material from a quotation. Ellipses consist of three spaced dots (. . .), with one space before and after each dot, used to indicate an omission (called the **ellipsis**) within quoted material. When using ellipses, type with spacing (. . .), NOT without (...). At the end of a sentence, a closely set final period precedes the ellipses (. . . at the end. . . .").

Based on a quotation taken from an article describing the messy offices of university faculty members (Yoe, p. 23), the examples below show how ellipses should be used. The complete quotation reads as follows:

> *"Call it nonlinear thinking. Call it creativity by association. Call it an aversion to throwing anything away. Whatever you call it and whatever its cause, you recognize the result: a mess."*

<u>When the beginning of a quotation is omitted</u>, begin the paragraph with a paragraph indention and 3 ellipsis dots:

> *" . . . nonlinear thinking. . . . creativity by association. . . . aversion to throwing anything away. Whatever you call it and whatever its cause, you recognize the result: a mess."*

<u>When the omission occurs within a sentence</u>, a space precedes and follows the ellipses:

> *"Call it nonlinear thinking. Call it creativity by association. Call it an aversion to throwing anything away. Whatever you call it . . . you recognize the result: a mess."*

If desirable, other punctuation may be added (in this example below, the comma that follows the omission has been retained) to further the sense of the sentence:

> *"Call it nonlinear thinking. Call it creativity. . . . Whatever you call it . . . , you recognize the result: a mess."*

<u>When the omission occurs after a complete sentence</u>, the ellipses follow the period, which is placed immediately after the last word in the sentence:

> *"Call it nonlinear thinking. . . . Call it an aversion to throwing anything away. Whatever you call it and whatever its cause, you recognize the result: a mess."*

In tables to indicate that no data were available

Ellipses may also be used in tables to indicate that no data were available or that a specific category of data does not apply (Iverson, p. 225).

This is the last chapter that includes exercises. The final chapter will discuss the end-of-sentence marks and selected issues of biomedical style.

1. She said, "The article has been accepted for publication in The Lancet."

   Which of the following should indicate the title of the journal?

   a. Italics.
   b. No punctuation.
   c. Single quotation marks.
   d. Double quotation marks.

2. **Which of the following statements is true?**

   a. A block quotation should begin and end with single quotation marks.
   b. A block quotation should begin and end with double quotation marks.
   c. A block quotation normally does not have quotation marks at the beginning or the end.
   d. A block quotation should be used for quoted material that consists of 2 or more sentences.

3. "Medicine can do only so much," said Dr. Perkins to his patient, "You will have to follow our recommendations if you hope to recover."

   What does this sentence need?

   a. No changes.
   b. The second comma replaced by a period.
   c. The first comma placed outside the closing quotation marks.
   d. The period after *recover* placed after the closing quotation marks.

4. The hospital association made a concerted effort this year to enact legislation that would have prohibited physician ownership of specialty, or so-called 'niche,' hospitals.

   What does this sentence need for correct punctuation?

   a. No punctuation changes.
   b. The comma after *niche* should be deleted.
   c. The single quotation marks around *niche* should be deleted.
   d. The single quotation marks around *niche* should be replaced with double quotation marks.

5. **The professor directed the students to the reference: "You can find the answer in the chapter Wedge and Shield Excision in your surgical textbook."**

How should the chapter title appear in this text?

a. In italics.
b. In single quotation marks.
c. In double quotation marks.
d. Simply as shown, with initial capital letters.

6. **He said the country's pharmaceutical sector is "totally unorganized . . . we do not have a national drug policy."**

What do the ellipses in this sentence indicate?

a. The writer was too lazy to include the entire quotation.
b. Material was omitted from the beginning of the next sentence.
c. The information on both sides of the ellipsis is taken from the same sentence.

Ending with Style

Sentences may close with a period, a question mark, or an exclamation point. "A question mark is stronger than a period; an exclamation point is stronger than a period or a question mark" (Sabin, p. 74).

The only marks that might follow these closing punctuation marks would be a closing parenthesis (if the entire sentence were parenthetical) or closing quotation marks (if the quotation completes the sentence).

> When a quoted sentence (a statement, a question, or an exclamation) falls at the end of a larger sentence, do not use double punctuation—that is, one mark to end the quotation and another to end the sentence. Choose the stronger mark. . . . If the same mark of punctuation is required for both the quotation and the sentence as a whole, use the one within quotation marks.

In the quotation above, what Sabin (p. 74) means by avoiding *double punctuation* is shown below:

INCORRECT: *The attendee asked, "Why are we here?".*

CORRECT: *The attendee asked, "Why are we here?"*

The period, the question mark, and the exclamation point serve specific functions. We'll look at these now.

THE PERIOD

Most sentences end with a period. The period is used to end a **declarative** or an **imperative sentence**. Examples of both types of sentences are shown below. In text, a single space follows the closing period.

Declarative: *Viewed grammatically, the period is stronger than a comma, a semicolon, or a colon.*

Imperative: *Feed the piranhas.*

Earlier (in Chapter 1) we looked at rearranging and rewriting as techniques for reducing punctuation and for fixing faulty sentence structure. As this pertains to the period, William Zinsser (p. 104) says it best:

> There's not much to be said about the period except that most writers don't reach it soon enough. If you find yourself hopelessly mired in a long sentence, it's probably because you are trying to make the sentence do more than it can reasonably do—perhaps express two dissimilar thoughts. The quickest way out is to break the long sentence into two short sentences, or even three.

The other most common use of the period is with certain abbreviations—but the styles for this use vary widely and change frequently. Just in my lifetime, I have seen an enormous shift from the use of periods after almost all abbreviations to the abolition of periods from most abbreviations, with certain exceptions. Abbreviations may appear in any of the following three forms (Chicago, p. 448; Iverson, p. 275):

Acronyms: terms based on the initial letters of the words in the expanded expression and read as single words (eg, *AIDS* for acquired immunodeficiency syndrome and *ELISA* for enzyme-linked immunosorbent assay)

Initialisms: terms read as a series of letters (eg, *WHO* for World Health Organization and *RN* for registered nurse)

Contractions: shortened terms that may include the first and last letters of the full word (eg, *Dr.* for "doctor" and *assn* for "association")

Although practices espoused by style manuals vary, on certain abbreviations we can find consensus. In scientific writing, abbreviated terms generally no longer end with periods (eg, *mL* **NOT** *mL.*). However, for abbreviated Latin terms such as *et al* (from *et alia*, meaning "and others") and *ie* (from *id est*, meaning "that is"), AMA deletes the periods but CBE retains them.

As we are discussing style related to abbreviations, note that AMA style uses a pair of commas to set off *Jr* and *Sr* when they follow a person's name but does not place a comma before a Roman numeral that follows a name (Iverson, p. 204):

AMA style: *Gerald B. Allen, Jr, MD, PhD*
BUT *Gerald B. Allen III, MD*

The CBE style is much more spare, using essentially no punctuation in names with abbreviations and titles. Elements that are set off with commas by AMA are separated by spaces by CBE (p. 186):

CBE style: *Gerald B Allen Sr MD FACP*

These are only a few of a number of stylistic differences between these two manuals. As style continues to change, I look forward to seeing what will happen to the period(s) after the initial(s) in a person's full name. These examples reinforce my strong recommendation that you become familiar with whatever style manual pertains to the work you are doing.

THE QUESTION MARK

Use a question mark to end an **interrogative sentence**:

Which regimen proved most effective?

"Place the question mark inside the end quotation mark, the closing parenthesis, or the end bracket when the question mark is part of the quoted or parenthetical material" (Iverson, p. 200).

The patient asked, "When may I expect to leave the hospital?"

The group (does this include the task force?) will meet on Friday.

In a declarative sentence containing an embedded question, the question mark is placed at the end of the question and is never combined with another question mark, exclamation point, period, semicolon, or comma:

The question, What will happen next? was on everyone's mind.

Sometimes, a question mark can change the tone of a sentence. Compare the following:

Declarative: *Would you mind feeding the piranhas.* (means *Feed the piranhas.*)

Interrogative: *Would you mind feeding the piranhas?* (means *It would be nice if you would feed the piranhas.*)

Also, the question mark may be used to indicate doubt about specific information or data.

THE EXCLAMATION POINT

An **exclamatory sentence** takes an exclamation point. Exclamation points are used to indicate emotion, an outcry, or a forceful comment. They appear rarely (but not necessarily never) in formal articles but may be used sometimes for emphasis in letters to the editor, book reviews, and editorials. The AMA advises restricting their use to direct quotations and "rare and special circumstances" (Iverson, p. 201). As William Zinsser (p. 105) puts it, "We have all suffered more than our share of these sentences in which an exclamation point knocks us over the head with how cute or wonderful something was. Instead, construct your sentence so that the order of the words will put the emphasis where you want it."

A FINAL WORD ON STYLE

Like our language, style undergoes constant change. Although not exerting too great an impact on the grammatical uses of punctuation that we have been considering in this workshop, style changes do involve punctuation marks. I have deliberately avoided pedantic emphasis on specific styles because of these continual mutations. As this module goes to press, new editions of both the AMA and CSE style manuals are nearing completion. So that you understand exactly how style changes affect punctuation, let's look at some examples of the changes anticipated in the forthcoming 10th edition of the AMA style manual (C. Iverson, written communication, February 2006):

◆ Fractions as nouns, previously not hyphenated, will now be hyphenated.

one-half to ***three-fourths*** *of the patients*

◆ Issue numbers, formerly not used in bibliographic entries for journals with consecutive pagination throughout a volume, will now be used (enclosed in parentheses) for all journals. For example,

JAMA. 1998;280(10):1909-1914.

◆ State names, formerly abbreviated after city names both in text and in references, will now be spelled out in text but abbreviated instead with the 2-letter postal codes in references.

A satellite clinic in Devon, **Pennsylvania***, was opened last year.*

Koop CE, Pearson CE, Schwarz MR, eds. *Critical Issues in Global Health.* San Francisco, **CA**: Jossey-Bass; 2002.

◆ The term "Available at:" will no longer be required for an electronic reference.

Our job is to know the conventions that pertain to our writing by keeping our style manuals handy and updated. That said, a final opinion from H. L. Mencken (p. 197) seems fitting for us to end this workshop on a balanced note:

> For the essence of a sound style is that it cannot be reduced to rules—that it is a living and breathing thing . . . —that it fits its proprietor tightly and yet ever so loosely, as his skin fits him. It is, in fact, quite as securely an integral part of him as that skin is. It hardens as his arteries harden. . . . To attempt to teach it is as silly as to set up courses in making love.

TAKE-HOME MESSAGES

Although we've covered considerable ground in this workshop, much more remains to be learned about punctuation. Education is a lifelong activity: we never stop learning. But so that we can conclude without your feeling overwhelmed, I'd like to leave you with a short list of points that will give you a firm foundation for using punctuation. I hope this review of salient points will serve to increase your confidence in applying punctuation effectively and to help you achieve the excellence to which we, as professionals, must aspire in our writing and editing:

- Punctuation defines <u>relationships</u> among elements in a sentence.

- Remember the four "C"s:

    Clarity
    Connectedness
    Conciseness
    Consistency

- A clause must have a subject <u>and</u> a predicate:

    Independent clause: can stand alone
    Dependent clause: can<u>not</u> stand alone

- Restrictive elements <u>cannot be omitted</u> without changing meaning; use the pronoun *that* and do <u>not</u> set off the elements with commas.

- <u>Nonrestrictive</u> elements <u>can be omitted</u> without changing meaning; use the pronoun *which* and set off the elements with a pair of commas.

- The clause before a colon <u>must be independent</u>.

- Dashes emphasize; parentheses de-emphasize.

- Use square brackets only <u>within</u> parentheses in text.

- Make exceptions when they support clarity!

- Consult style manuals and dictionaries.

Thank you for taking this workshop. I hope that this module and what you have learned will prove useful for you. Good luck in your future professional development.

Always eager to improve its educational offerings, AMWA welcomes your comments and suggestions about its courses. Please feel free to send these to the association's headquarters:

American Medical Writers Association
40 West Gude Drive, Suite 101
Rockville, MD 20850-1192
Telephone: (301) 294-5303
Fax: (301) 294-9006
E-mail: amwa@amwa.org
Web address: www.amwa.org

Glossary

Acronyms: Terms based on the initial letters of the words in the expanded expression and read as single words (eg, *AIDS* for "acquired immunodeficiency syndrome" and *ELISA* for "enzyme-linked immunosorbent assay").

Apostrophe: A punctuation mark used to indicate the omission of letters or figures, the possessive case, and the plural of some letters or figures.

Appositive: "A noun or noun phrase that identifies another noun or pronoun that immediately precedes it" (Sabin, p. 636).

Aside: An inaudible utterance or a digression from the theme.

Brackets: A pair of punctuation marks ([ ]) used in writing and printing to enclose matter or in mathematics and logic as signs of aggregation.

Clause: A group of words that contains a subject and a predicate.

Close punctuation: The tendency to use "as many marks as the grammatical construction will justify" (Skillin, p. 184).

Colon: A punctuation mark used chiefly to direct attention to matter that follows.

Comma: A mark of separation within a sentence.

Complement: A word that appears in the predicate and is needed to complete the sense of the verb.

Complex sentence: A sentence consisting of one independent clause and at least one dependent clause.

Compound predicate: Two or more predicates joined by conjunctions.

Compound sentence: A sentence consisting of two or more independent clauses.

Compound subject: Two or more subjects of the same verb in a sentence.

Compound-complex sentence: A sentence consisting of at least two independent clauses and one or more dependent clauses.

Conjunction: A word that joins other words or groups of words (see **Coordinating** and **Subordinating**).

Conjunctive adverb: A word that can be used with a semicolon and a comma to join two independent clauses into a single sentence.

Contraction: A shortened form of a word or phrase in which an apostrophe indicates the omitted letters or words.

Coordinate adjectives: Two or more adjectives that modify the same noun.

Coordinating conjunction: A word that connects words, phrases, or clauses of equal rank (eg, *for*, *and*, *nor*, *but*, *or*, *yet*, and *so*).

Dash: A mark of internal punctuation that is used to indicate a break in the thought or structure of a sentence (see **Em dash** and **En dash**).

Dependent clause: A clause that cannot stand alone but depends on the rest of the sentence for its meaning.

Declarative sentence: A sentence that makes a statement.

Direct object: The person or thing that receives the action of the verb or upon which the action of the verb is performed.

Direct quotation: The exact words taken directly from another source.

Ellipses: Three spaced dots, with one space before and after each, used to indicate an omission within quoted material.

Ellipsis: An omission within quoted material.

Elliptical construction: A phrasing in which one or more words have been purposely omitted because they can be readily inferred.

Em dash: A dash equal to the width of the capital letter "M."

En dash: A dash equal to the width of the capital letter "N."

Eponyms: "Phrases or names derived from or including the name of a person or place" (Iverson, p. 469).

Exclamatory sentence: A sentence that expresses strong feeling.

Gerund: The *-ing* form of a verb that is used as a noun.

Hyphen: A punctuation mark used to divide or to compound words, word elements, or numbers (see **Orthographic** and **Temporary**).

Imperative sentence: A sentence that expresses a command or a request.

Independent clause: A clause that can stand alone to express a complete thought.

Indirect quotation: A rephrased statement of another source's exact words, often introduced by words such as *whether, when,* or *that.*

Indirect object: The person or thing on whose behalf, to whom, or for whom the action of the verb is performed.

Infinitive: The form of a verb that includes the word *to.*

Initialisms: Terms read as a series of letters (eg, *WHO* for "World Health Organization" and *RN* for "registered nurse").

Interrogative sentence: A sentence that asks a question.

Intransitive verb: A verb that does not require a complement or an object to complete its meaning.

Linking verb: A verb that does not express action but rather shows a state of being.

Nonrestrictive elements: Words, phrases, or clauses that are not needed to complete the meaning of a sentence.

Open punctuation: Use of only as much punctuation as is absolutely necessary for clarity.

Orthographic hyphens: Hyphens that are part of the accepted spelling of a word.

Parentheses: The curved marks used to enclose a parenthetical expression or to group a symbolic unit in a logical or mathematical expression.

Participial phrase: A group of words formed by a participle and the words related to it.

Participle: A verb form used as an adjective.

Phrase: A group of words that does not contain a subject and a predicate.

Possessive case: The case taken by a noun or pronoun when it is used to show possession or ownership.

Predicate: The verb in the sentence plus all of the words that relate to the verb.

Prepositional phrase: A group of words consisting of a preposition plus its object and any words that modify the object.

Relative clause: A dependent clause introduced by a relative pronoun and referring or relating to an earlier word in the sentence.

Relative pronoun: A pronoun that relates to a noun (antecedent) preceding it in the sentence and that introduces a relative clause (ie, *who, which,* or *that*).

Restrictive elements: Words, phrases, or clauses that are necessary for the meaning of the sentence.

Semicolon: A punctuation mark used chiefly to serve a coordinating function between independent clauses.

Sentence: A group of words containing a subject and a predicate and expressing a complete thought; a sentence will always be an independent clause, but not every independent clause will be a sentence (sentences often contain several clauses). (See **Simple, Compound, Complex, Compound-complex, Declarative, Exclamatory, Imperative,** and **Interrogative.**)

Serial comma: The comma used before the coordinating conjunction *and* that precedes the final item in a series.

Series: Three or more items of the same class coming one after the other in succession.

Simple sentence: A sentence consisting of a single independent clause.

Slash: The punctuation mark (also called a **virgule**) used mainly to symbolize the phrase *divided by* or *per* in mathematical expressions.

Square brackets: A pair of punctuation marks used in writing and printing to enclose matter or in mathematics and logic as signs of aggregation.

Subject: The person or thing that performs the action of the verb or is in the state of being described by the verb.

Subordinating conjunction: A conjunction that joins elements of unequal weight or importance (eg, *however, although, while, because, if,* and *since*).

Temporary hyphens: Hyphens used to form compounds when relationships among words need to be clarified.

Transitional expressions: Expressions that link independent clauses or sentences (eg, *in contrast, however, thus,* and *nevertheless*).

Transitive verb: A verb that requires a direct object to complete its meaning.

Verb: A part of speech showing action or a state of being (see **Transitive** and **Intransitive**).

Virgule: The punctuation mark used mainly to symbolize the phrase *divided by* or *per* in mathematical expressions (see **Slash**).

Bibliography

Allen JS. Educating performers. *The Key Reporter*. Spring 1992:5–9.

Benbow J. *Manuscript & Proof*. New York, NY: Oxford University Press; 1938:92.

Cowper W. The Task, Book II, The Timepiece, line 606. In: Bartlett J. *Familiar Quotations*. 13th ed. Boston, MA: Little Brown & Co; 1955:364a.

The Chicago Manual of Style. 15th ed. Chicago, IL and London, UK: The University of Chicago Press; 2003.

Style Manual Committee, Council of Biology Editors. *Scientific Style and Format: The CBE Manual for Authors, Editors, and Publishers*. 6th ed. Cambridge, UK: Cambridge University Press; 1994.

Dorland's Illustrated Medical Dictionary. 30th ed. Philadelphia, PA: WB Saunders Co; 2003.

Huth EJ. *Medical Style and Format: An International Manual for Authors, Editors, and Publishers*. Philadelphia, PA: ISI Press; 1987.

Iverson C, Chair, AMA Style Manual Committee. *American Medical Association Manual of Style*. 9th ed. Baltimore, MD: Williams and Wilkins; 1998.

Kelly EH. Art. VI.—On the treatment of ulcers, and certain cutaneous affections. *The New Orleans Medical and Surgical Journal*. 1846; II:40.

Knatterud ME. Punctuation for Clarity and Style. In: Witte FM, Taylor ND, eds. *Essays for Biomedical Communicators: Volume 1 of Selected AMWA Workshops*. Rockville, MD: American Medical Writers Association; 2001.

Mencken HL. Literature and the Schoolma'm. In: *Prejudices: Fifth Series*. New York, NY: Alfred A. Knopf, Inc; 1926.

Merriam-Webster's Collegiate Dictionary. 11th ed. Springfield, MA: Merriam-Webster, Inc; 2004.

Sabin WA. *The Gregg Reference Manual*. 10th ed. New York, NY: Glencoe McGraw-Hill; 2005.

Schwager E. *Medical English Usage and Abusage*. Phoenix, AZ: Oryx Press; 1991.

Skillin M, Gay RM. *Words into Type*. 3rd ed. Upper Saddle River, NJ: Prentice Hall; 1974.

Stedman's Medical Dictionary. 27th ed. Philadelphia, PA: Lippincott Williams & Wilkins; 2000.

Stilman A. *Grammatically Correct: The Writer's Essential Guide to Punctuation, Spelling, Usage and Grammar*. Cincinnati, OH: Writer's Digest Books; 1997.

Truss L. *Eats, Shoots & Leaves: The Zero Tolerance Approach to Punctuation*. London, GB; 2003.

Witte F. *Basic Grammar and Usage for Biomedical Communicators: A Core Curriculum Workshop of the American Medical Writers Association*. Dubuque, IA: Kendall/Hunt Publishing Co; 2003.

Woolever KR. *Writing for the Technical Professions*. 3rd ed. New York, NY: Pearson/Longman; 2003.

Yoe MR. Kings of Chaos. *University of Chicago Magazine*. 2001; 93(5):23–31.

Zeiger M. *Essentials of Writing Biomedical Research Papers*. New York, NY: McGraw-Hill, Inc; 1991.

Zinsser W. *On Writing Well*. 2nd ed. New York, NY: Harper & Row; 1980.

1. a. Very good! These participial phrases modify the subject.
   b. Sorry! These are neither dependent nor clauses. Try again.
   c. Sorry! These phrases contain prepositions, but they are not prepositional phrases. Try again.
   d. Sorry! The predicate contains only one verb, *were characterized;* furthermore, these elements modify the noun *events* and are not part of the predicate. Try again.

2. a. Sorry! A simple sentence consists of a single independent clause. Try again.
   b. Sorry! A complex sentence consists of one independent clause and at least one dependent clause. Try again.
   c. Sorry! A compound sentence contains two independent clauses. Try again.
   d. Good! A compound-complex sentence consists of at least two independent clauses (*she was treated also for a kidney infection* and *she was released after 2 weeks*) and one or more dependent clauses (*While the patient was hospitalized for the hypotension*).

3. a. Sorry! This element is not a clause because it does not contain a subject. Try again.
   b. Sorry! This element contains more than the direct object of the verb. Try again.
   c. Good! This predicate consists of a transitive verb and multiple direct objects.
   d. Sorry! This sentence has no indirect object. Try again.

4. a. Sorry! Other punctuation is needed. Try again.
   b. Sorry! This punctuation does not clarify relationships. Try again.
   c. Sorry! This punctuation does not clarify relationships. Try again.
   d. Good! This punctuation clarifies the problems being relieved.

5. a. Sorry! The predicate contains only one verb and, thus, is not compound. Try again.
   b. Very good! This relative clause modifies the subject with restrictive information. The relative pronoun *that* introduces the adjectival clause that modifies the noun *endoscopes.*
   c. Sorry! The information in this element restricts the meaning of the sentence. Try again.
   d. Sorry! This element is not a phrase because it contains a subject and a verb. Try again.

6. a. Sorry! This sentence does not contain a participle. Try again.
   b. Very good! This is a dependent clause: as a clause, this element has a subject and a predicate but the clause is dependent because it cannot stand alone.
   c. Sorry! This is not an independent clause. Try again.
   d. Sorry! Containing a subject and a verb, this element is not a phrase. Try again.

7. a. Good! Both are linking verbs.
   b. Sorry! These verbs do not take an object, as transitive verbs must. Try again.
   c. Sorry! The sentence does not contain a participle. Try again.
   d. Sorry! The predicate is incomplete with the verbs alone. Try again.

8. a. Sorry! This is an independent clause. Try again
   b. Sorry! This is an independent clause. Try again.
   c. Sorry! This is a prepositional phrase. Try again.
   d. Very good! You have identified the dependent clause.

9. a. Sorry! A predicate contains the verb in the sentence. Try again.
   b. Good! A linking verb, like *is* in this sentence, takes a complement.
   c. Sorry! A direct object follows a transitive verb. Try again.
   d. Sorry! This sentence contains no indirect object. Try again.

10. a. Very good! This subject is a gerund phrase. A gerund is the *-ing* form of a verb that functions as a noun.
    b. Sorry! This is not the predicate of any of the three independent clauses in this sentence. Try again.
    c. Sorry! A clause must have both a subject and a predicate. Try again.
    d. Sorry! A clause must have both a subject and a predicate. Try again.

1. a. Sorry! Two independent clauses joined by a coordinating conjunction require a comma. Try again.
    b. Good! The comma should be placed <u>before</u>, not after, the coordinating conjunction.
    c. Sorry! The two independent clauses are not separated correctly.

2. a. Sorry! A comma after *all* separates elements in the introductory phrase that belong together. Try again.
    b. Very good! A comma after *above* clarifies relationships here.
    c. Sorry! Placing a comma between *studies* and *above* would distort the meaning and confuse the reader. Try again.
    d. Sorry! This sentence begins with a phrase, not a clause. Try again.

3. a. Sorry! The sentence needs the addition of one comma. Try again.
    b. Sorry! Placing a comma after *amino acids* would separate these prepositional phrases that modify the verb *determined*. Try again.
    c. Very good! A comma is indicated before the conjunction introducing the third element in the series.

4. a. Sorry! The sentence needs additional punctuation. Try again.
    b. Very good! A comma would separate correctly the introductory dependent clause from the independent clause.
    c. Sorry! Setting off *more and more* with a pair of commas would introduce ambiguity: should this phrase modify the introductory dependent clause, or should the phrase modify the subject (*bronchial damage*) of the independent clause? Try again.
    d. Sorry! A comma <u>is</u> needed to separate an introductory dependent clause from an independent clause. Try again.

5. a. Sorry! Additional punctuation is needed. Try again.
    b. Sorry! The two objects of the preposition *between* do not need to be separated for clarity here; the adjectives following the coordinating conjunction (*and*) should eliminate the possibility of reading this as *environmental factors and genetic,* which would make no sense. The second object (*genetic and acquired susceptibility*) can be read easily as a unit without being set off. Try again.
    c. Good! A comma belongs after the transitional expression *Conversely.*
    d. Sorry! A comma between the two independent clauses is correct because they <u>are</u> joined by a coordinating conjunction. Try again.

6. a. Sorry! This sentence contains a punctuation error. Try again.
   b. Very good! This is a compound predicate, and punctuation should not separate the subject from either of its two verbs.
   c. Sorry! The prepositional phrase *in the southwestern United States* is restrictive and should not be set off from the rest of the sentence. Try again.

7. a. Very good! The sentence is punctuated correctly.
   b. Sorry! This serial comma is certainly needed here. Try again.
   c. Sorry! A comma should not be used to separate the subject (*data from returned questionnaires*) from its second verb (*reviewed*) in this compound predicate. Try again.

8. a. Sorry! This sentence needs internal punctuation. Try again.
   b. Sorry! Do not separate the subject of this dependent clause, *antibodies,* from its verb, *play,* by using a single comma. Try again.
   c. Good! *Although present,* which is nonrestrictive and interrupts the flow of the sentence, is set off properly by a pair of commas.
   d. Sorry! This prepositional phrase does not need to be set off. Try again.

9. a. Sorry! This sentence needs additional punctuation. Try again.
   b. Good! A comma should be placed between the coordinate adjectives *difficult* and *time-consuming*.
   c. Sorry! The introductory participial phrase must be separated from the independent clause. The sentence would otherwise not be clear. Try again.

1. a. Sorry! The sentence is not punctuated correctly. Try again.
    b. Good! Semicolons should be used between elements in an enumeration when at least one item contains a comma.
    c. Sorry! The semicolon following *membranes* is correct as written. Try again.
    d. Sorry! A semicolon should not be used to introduce an enumeration. Try again.

2. a. Sorry! The sentence is not punctuated correctly. Try again.
    b. Sorry! A comma <u>is</u> needed, but this is not the best answer. Try again.
    c. Sorry! A semicolon <u>is</u> needed, but this is not the best answer. Try again.
    d. Good! A semicolon separates correctly the two independent clauses, and a comma is needed after the conjunctive adverb *therefore*.

3. a. Sorry! The sentence is not punctuated properly. Try again.
    b. Very good! Semicolons are needed to separate the elements in this enumeration because one element has an internal comma.
    c. Sorry! This comma should not be deleted because it correctly sets off the nonrestrictive phrase *including swimwear*. Try again.
    d. Sorry! The colon <u>is</u> the mark of choice here to introduce the enumeration. Try again.

4. a. Sorry! The comma is used correctly to set off an introductory phrase. Try again.
    b. Sorry! The semicolon is used correctly here. Try again.
    c. Sorry! This is not a correct reason. Try again.
    d. Very good! The semicolon is used because no coordinating conjunction joins these two independent clauses.

5. a. Very good! This compound sentence is punctuated correctly.
    b. Sorry! A semicolon is not used when a coordinating conjunction separates two independent clauses. Try again.
    c. Sorry! Remember that a comma separates two independent clauses joined by a coordinating conjunction. Try again.

6. a. Sorry! The punctuation needs to be changed. Try again.
    b. Sorry! This is not the best answer. Try again.
    c. Good! A semicolon correctly separates two independent clauses joined by a conjunctive adverb, which should be followed by a comma.
    d. Sorry! This is not the best answer. Try again.

7. a. Sorry! Changes would improve this text. Try again.
   b. Very good! The first and second clauses belong together and should be linked more closely than as two separate sentences.
   c. Sorry! Between the second and third independent clauses is not the best place for a semicolon because the first and second, pertaining to a specific doctor, belong together; the third sentence is a general statement. Try again.
   d. Sorry! Connecting all three independent clauses with semicolons would make the content less clear. Try again.

8. a. Sorry! Clarifying the relationships among these clauses requires changes in punctuation. Try again.
   b. Sorry! Although not incorrect, a period would make too strong a break between these two clauses and would not be the best punctuation for this sentence. Try again.
   c. Very good! The sense of this sentence mandates a semicolon after *planes* to show the close relationship between these two clauses and to clarify the meaning by indicating that the dependent clause *if a transverse problem is apparent* pertains to the indication for additional analysis.
   d. Sorry! This would be an improper place for a semicolon because the dependent clause pertains to the independent clause that follows. Try again.

1. a. Sorry! The sentence contains an error. Try again.
    b. Good! No colon should be used because the sentence is continuous and the colon would separate a linking verb (*were*) from its complement; also, because the material before the colon is not a complete sentence (or an independent clause).
    c. Sorry! A colon is not always used to introduce an enumeration. Try again.
    d. Sorry! The commas are appropriate for these serial items. Try again.

2. a. Good! The colon follows an independent clause and introduces the listed items.
    b. Sorry! A period is too strong to effectively mark the relationship between the first independent clause and those that it introduces. Try again.
    c. Sorry! A comma is not adequate here. Try again.
    d. Sorry! A semicolon does not introduce an enumeration. Try again.

3. a. Sorry! The sentence contains an error. Try again.
    b. Sorry! The construction of this sentence does not call for a comma to introduce the formal quotation. Try again.
    c. Sorry! A semicolon is not appropriate to introduce this formal quotation. Try again.
    d. Very good! The colon is the appropriate mark to introduce this formal quotation.

4. a. Very good! The colon is used appropriately when the second independent clause develops, amplifies, or details the first.
    b. Sorry! A period would weaken the relationship between these two clauses. Try again.
    c. Sorry! A comma is inadequate to separate two independent clauses in the absence of a coordinating conjunction. Try again.
    d. Sorry! A semicolon is not the best choice here. Try again.

5. a. Sorry! The punctuation is not entirely correct. Try again.
    b. Sorry! A period should follow the list of authors. Try again.
    c. Sorry! The semicolon correctly separates the year from the volume number. Try again.
    d. Good! A colon correctly separates the volume number from the page numbers.

6. a. Sorry! The sentence contains an error. Try again.
    b. Sorry! The colon separates the preposition *of* from its objects. Try again.
    c. Good! A preposition should not be separated from its objects.
    d. Sorry! The commas correctly separate the items in the series. Try again.

7. a. Good! A colon should be used after an independent clause that suggests "the following."
    b. Sorry! A period would leave phrases dangling. Try again.
    c. Sorry! A comma would make this sentence unclear and would distort the intended meaning. Try again.
    d. Sorry! A semicolon would leave phrases dangling. Try again.

8. a. Sorry! The relationship between these two clauses does not call for a colon. Try again.
    b. Sorry! A period would weaken the relationship between these two clauses. Try again.
    c. Sorry! A comma is inadequate to separate two independent clauses in the absence of a coordinating conjunction. Try again.
    d. Very good! The semicolon correctly separates these two independent clauses in the absence of a coordinating conjunction. A colon would be used only if the second clause amplified or developed the first; the second clause here is more parallel than explanatory.

9. a. Good! No colon is used when the sentence is continuous.
    b. Sorry! A colon should not separate a conjunction from subsequent clauses. Try again.
    c. Sorry! A comma should not separate a conjunction from subsequent clauses. Try again.
    d. Sorry! A semicolon is definitely not indicated here. Try again.

10. a. Sorry! The sentence contains an error. Try again.
    b. Sorry! A dash is not the correct punctuation mark here. Try again.
    c. Good! The colon follows an independent clause and introduces a list.
    d. Sorry! The sentence contains only one main clause. Try again.

11. a. Sorry! Hyphens are not used to express numeric ratios. Try again.
    b. Good! The colons correctly express these ratios.
    c. Sorry! This is not the best way to express a ratio. Try again.

1. a. Sorry! An en dash is not used to set off introductory elements. Try again.
   b. Sorry! An em dash is used to precede a name in an attribution. Try again.
   c. Sorry! An em dash is used to provide rhythmic and visual variety.
   d. Good! Showing relational distinction in compound words is an important function of the en dash.

2. a. Very good! Spelling out the prepositions indicates to the reader whether the range is exclusive or inclusive. In this sentence, the reader is being told that the range begins in 1979 and extends up to but does not include the year 2000.
   b. Sorry! The en dash should not be used in a range in running text. Try again.
   c. Sorry! An em dash is not used between two dates. Try again.
   d. Sorry! We have no reason to think that the range is inclusive, so changing the preposition to make it so is not indicated. Try again.

3. a. Sorry! Em dashes are used correctly in running text. Try again.
   b. Sorry! Showing relational distinction in compound words is a function of the en dash. Try again.
   c. Good! Em dashes are used correctly with appositive and parenthetic expressions.
   d. Sorry! Em dashes are not used between consecutive numbers in lists and tables, in or out of running text. Try again.

4. a. Good! An en dash is used for a minus symbol.
   b. Sorry! An em dash is not used for a minus symbol. Try again.
   c. Sorry! A two-em dash is not the appropriate mark for a minus symbol. Try again.
   d. Sorry! A three-em dash is not the appropriate mark for a minus symbol. Try again.

5. a. Sorry! An en dash is not used to indicate missing letters. Try again.
   b. Sorry! An em dash is not used to indicate missing letters. Try again.
   c. Good! A two-em dash is the proper mark for indicating missing letters.
   d. Sorry! A three-em dash is used to indicate a missing word, not missing letters. Try again.

6. a. Good! The em dash is used to indicate and emphasize the break in thought.
   b. Sorry! A comma would not effectively mark the interruption in flow at this point in the sentence. Try again.
   c. Sorry! The comma correctly sets off the modifying phrase *understood as each person's receiving his or her share of a valuable social resource held in common.* An em dash after *fairness* would be inappropriately interrupt the flow of the sentence. Try again.
   d. Sorry! The phrase between *fairness* and *medical* modifies the independent clause in the sentence and should not be set off by a pair of en dashes. Try again.

7. a. Sorry! The relationship among the elements in the subject needs to be clarified. Try again.
    b. Sorry! A comma at this point in the sentence does not really clarify the relationships in the subject. Try again.
    c. Sorry! An en dash at this point in the sentence would be incorrect. Try again.
    d. Very good! A pair of em dashes will clarify the relationships in the subject by setting off the parenthetic information *calcium or magnesium or both.*

8. a. Sorry! A colon must be preceded by an independent clause. Try again.
    b. Sorry! A comma would be incorrect. Try again.
    c. Very good! The em dash would be used properly here to set off an introductory series from the clause that sums up its elements.
    d. Sorry! A semicolon should be placed between two independent clauses; this sentence has only one. Try again.

9. a. Sorry! Criteria for colon use are not met here. Try again.
    b. Sorry! Criteria for en dash use are not present. Try again.
    c. Good! An em dash indicates the sudden interruption in the flow of the sentence.
    d. Sorry! A semicolon requires two independent clauses. Try again.

10. a. Sorry! A comma could be used here, but it would not be the most effective choice because the summarizing phrase at the end would tend to get lost. Try again.
    b. Sorry! An en dash would be an inappropriate punctuation mark here. Try again.
    c. Good! An em dash will provide clarity and emphasis in the sentence.
    d. Sorry! A semicolon would be an inappropriate punctuation mark here. Try again.

11. a. Sorry! A comma is not correct. Try again.
    b. Very good! An en dash is the appropriate mark to link the unhyphenated compound (*sickle cell*) and the second condition (*thalassemia*) that together modify *disease.*
    c. Sorry! An em dash is not correct. Try again.
    d. Sorry! A punctuation mark is needed. Try again.

1. a. Sorry! This sentence contains multiple punctuation errors. Try again.
    b. Sorry! The nonrestrictive phrases in this sentence are not punctuated consistently. Try again.
    c. Sorry! A comma should not precede the restrictive relative clause. Try again.
    d. Good! Both parenthetic phrases are nonrestrictive.

2. a. Sorry! This sentence can be improved. Try again.
    b. Sorry! The second comma incorrectly separates this compound subject. Try again.
    c. Very good! Raw numbers should be given primacy, and parenthetic percentages should follow.
    d. Sorry! Yes, the numbers should precede the percentages, but a four-digit numeral should be solid, with no punctuation. Try again.

3. a. Sorry! This sentence contains an error. Try again.
    b. Very good! Punctuation does not precede an opening parenthesis, except for parenthetic numerals in an enumeration.
    c. Sorry! A comma separating the subject (*fungi*) from its verb (*cause*) would be incorrect. Try again.
    d. Sorry! The names of these species are supplementary, nonrestrictive information. Dashes are not necessary. Try again.

4. a. Sorry! A term must be spelled before it is abbreviated. Try again.
    b. Sorry! The associations mentioned are nonrestrictive and need to be enclosed by parentheses. Try again.
    c. Very good! Parenthetic information within parenthetic information should be placed in square brackets.
    d. Sorry! Square brackets should be placed within parentheses. Try again.

5. a. Very good! The quoted speaker used only the abbreviation; the editor has inserted the full name for readers who do not recognize the abbreviation. The square brackets indicate that the full name is an editorial addition and not part of the original quotation.
    b. Sorry! Parentheses would not be appropriate here. Try again.
    c. Sorry! This International System of Units (SI) expression is expressed correctly within parentheses, following the traditional metric system expression. Try again.
    d. Sorry! Ordinarily, a parenthetic abbreviation follows a full term, but because this is part of a quotation, we cannot just rearrange and add information as if it were part of the original quotation. Try again.

6. a. Sorry! Errors exist in this sentence. Try again.
    b. Sorry! The word *workforce* is an unhyphenated compound. Try again.
    c. Sorry! The word *its* is a possessive pronoun, which does not need an apostrophe. Try again.
    d. Very good! To correct this sentence, the comma after *smoke* and the period <u>before</u> the closing parenthesis should be deleted, and a period should be placed <u>after</u> the closing parenthesis.

Welcome to the American Medical Writers Association's (AMWA's) self-study module, *Punctuation for Clarity and Style*. We hope that you will find this module instructive and easy to use. *Punctuation for Clarity and Style* is **the second in a series of computer-based workshops** created to further AMWA's ongoing efforts to help you achieve excellence in medical communication. The workshop is designed for writers and editors at all levels of experience—from those seeking to improve their punctuation skills to those seeking to refresh them. The workbook is intended to serve as a valuable reference guide long after the course has been completed.

Punctuation for Clarity and Style is one of the cornerstone workshops of **AMWA's certificate program**—an extensive continuing education program for professional communicators in the medical and allied scientific fields. Some employers require the certificate, which is considered part of a career path in the field. Workshops are offered in 5 specialty areas (editing/writing, pharmaceutical, freelance, educators, and public relations/advertising/marketing). A **core certificate** may be earned by satisfactorily completing 4 general workshops plus 4 elective workshops from 1 of the 5 specialty areas. A **multidisciplinary certificate** requires satisfactory completion of 4 general workshops plus 6 elective workshops from 3 or more specialty areas. Workshops are offered at chapter conferences throughout the year and at AMWA's annual conference in the fall. More information about the certificate program and about AMWA in general can be found on AMWA's Web site: **www.amwa.org**.

If you would like to receive certificate credit for completing this module, **you must first enroll** in the program by completing the enrollment form that can be found at AMWA's Web site (under Education/Certificates) or can be ordered from AMWA headquarters. You will also need to submit the enrollment fee with your completed form. Please note that you do not have to take this course for credit; however, if you do want credit, you must first enroll.

In this workbook you will find an **answer sheet to be used for taking the final examination**. Once you have completed the module and the examination, mail your answer sheet to AMWA headquarters for scoring (a passing score is 85%). You will receive a pass/fail notification; your answer sheet will not be returned to you. Please note that only the purchaser of this module is eligible for credit. Answer sheets submitted by persons who are not on record with AMWA headquarters as having purchased this module will be discarded. Participants who earn a passing score on the examination and who are enrolled in the core certificate program will receive credit. Those who do not earn a passing score may request a new answer sheet and take the examination again by submitting a $50 payment to AMWA headquarters.

Thank you for purchasing this module. If you have comments or suggestions about this course, please send them to AMWA headquarters at the address above or at the following e-mail address: dane@amwa.org.

1. a. Sorry! A change is needed. Try again.
    b. Good! These two words are hyphenated to form a single unit that precedes and modifies the description of the *T lymphocytes*.
    c. Sorry! These elements do not precede a noun and, therefore, should not be hyphenated. Try again.

2. a. Very good! The hyphenation is correct.
    b. Sorry! A Latin expression or other foreign expression is not hyphenated, even when used as an adjectival modifier. Try again.
    c. Sorry! The hyphen correctly joins a compound in which the first element is a number and the compound precedes the noun it modifies, *life span*.

3. a. Sorry! Punctuation is needed. Try again.
    b. Sorry! More punctuation is needed. Try again.
    c. Sorry! This is not the best punctuation. Try again.
    d. Very good! The en dash joins the hyphenated unit *B-cell* with the past participle *depleted* to form the larger unit that modifies *fraction*.

4. a. Sorry! This hyphenation is not correct. Try again.
    b. Sorry! This hyphenation is not correct. Try again.
    c. Sorry! Still more punctuation is needed. Try again.
    d. Good! Hyphens after both numbers join them with the unit of measure *mL* to form the compound that modifies *sample*.

5. a. Sorry! The slash is not appropriate between two separate individuals. Try again.
    b. Good! The hyphen correctly joins this compound of two nouns of equal participation.
    c. Sorry! The en dash is not appropriate. Try again.

6. a. Good. No hyphen is needed because *calcium deficient* follows the subject it modifies. In this sentence, *calcium deficient* serves as the complement of the noun *patient*.
    b. Sorry! The hyphen is not needed.Try again.

7. a. Sorry! A sentence should not begin with a numeral. Try again.
    b. Sorry! This hyphenation is not correct. Try again.
    c. Sorry! This hyphenation is not correct. Try again.
    d. Good! Written numbers above 99 (*one hundred*) are not hyphenated, but those from 21 through 99 are.

8. a. Good! The prefix *intra* combines usually without a hyphen.
    b. Sorry! The hyphen is not correct. Try again.
    c. Sorry! The prefix *intra* cannot stand alone. Try again.

9. a. Sorry! A prefix should not form a solid word with a proper noun. Try again.
    b. Good! The hyphen correctly joins the prefix *post* with the proper noun *Holocaust*.
    c. Sorry! A change is needed. Try again.

10. a. Good. No hyphens are needed with either the prefix *pre* or the suffix *wide*.
    b. Sorry! The last two words in the sentence should be connected. Try again.
    c. Sorry! The hyphen is not correct. Try again.

11. a. Sorry! Hyphenation is needed. Try again.
    b. Very good! In this hyphenated compound, both *age* and *sex* share the common base *adjusted*, which is omitted properly after *age*. *Relative-prevalence* is a temporary compound that modifies the noun it precedes, *ratios*.
    c. Sorry! The sentence needs more changes. Try again.

1. a. Good! The singular possessive is formed with an apostrophe plus the letter *s*.
   b. Sorry! The plural noun followed by the apostrophe forms a plural possessive. Try again.

2. a. Good! A possessive pronoun has no apostrophe.
   b. Sorry! This is not a contraction. Try again.

3. a. Sorry! This would be a singular test's result. Try again.
   b. Good! The letter *s* after the abbreviation indicates multiple procedures, and the final apostrophe makes them possessive.
   c. Sorry! This is not the correct formation for a plural possessive. Try again.

4. a. Good! Current usage indeed favors the nonpossessive form of eponyms, omitting the apostrophe and the letter *s*.
   b. Sorry! This form is correct but has fallen out of favor. Try again.
   c. Sorry! The man's name is Gram, not Grams. Try again.
   d. Sorry! Gram's name should not be treated as a plural. Try again.

5. a. Very good! A single apostrophe is used only after the final name in joint possession.
   b. Sorry! This is not correct punctuation for a joint possessive. Try again.

6. a. Sorry! The noun *months* is plural in this sentence. Try again.
   b. Good! A plural possessive uses an apostrophe after the plural form of the noun.

7. a. Sorry! The scores are not held jointly as this punctuation implies. Try again.
   b. Good! In cases of separate possession, each noun takes its own apostrophe.
   c. Sorry! *Men* and *women* are already plural without a final *s*. Try again.

8. a. Sorry! The slash construction is not preferred in running text. Try again.
   b. Good! The slash construction should not be used in running text.
   c. Sorry! One construction is preferred over the other. Try again.

9. a. Good! The slash is not used when a prepositional phrase intervenes between the two elements (*IU* and *d*).
   b. Sorry. This expression is acceptable because the slash is not used. Try again.
   c. Sorry! This expression is acceptable. Try again.

10. a. Sorry! The options are presented more clearly without the *and/or* construction. Try again.
    b. Good! As a rule, avoid the *and/or* construction in text.

1. a. Good! Titles of complete works are expressed in italics.
    b. Sorry! Further punctuation is needed. Try again.
    c. Sorry! Single quotation marks are not correct. Try again.
    d. Sorry! Double quotation marks are not correct. Try again.

2. a. Sorry! Single quotation marks are used only for quotations within quotations. Try again.
    b. Sorry! Double quotation marks are not correct. Try again.
    c. Good! The block indentation removes the need for quotation marks.
    d. Sorry! Block form is used correctly for quotations longer than 4 lines. Try again.

3. a. Sorry! An error needs to be corrected. Try again.
    b. Good! A period should follow *patient*. The quoted material that continues must be a new sentence because no coordinating conjunction separates the two quoted independent clauses.
    c. Sorry! The comma after *much* correctly sets off what is being said from the person who is saying it. Try again.
    d. Sorry! American style calls for the period to be placed within the closing quotation marks. Try again.

4. a. Sorry! A change is needed. Try again.
    b. Sorry! The appositive phrase *or so-called niche* is set off properly with the pair of commas. Try again.
    c. Good! Quotation marks are not used with words that follow *so-called.*
    d. Sorry! Neither single nor double quotation marks are correct. Try again.

5. a. Sorry! Italics are not correct for a chapter title. Try again.
    b. Very good! Although double quotation marks would otherwise be indicated, this chapter title needs to be enclosed by single quotation marks because it appears within a quotation.
    c. Sorry! In this sentence, double quotation marks are not correct. Try again.
    d. Sorry! This title needs punctuation. Try again.

6. a. Sorry! We don't know this. Try again.
    b. Sorry! Three ellipsis points alone do not indicate an omission at the end of a sentence. Try again.
    c. Good! The three ellipsis points do indicate an omission within a sentence.

Index

Final Examination

Select the best answer (according to AMA style) for each question from the choices that follow.

1. <u>These low molecular weight materials</u> can elicit delayed hypersensitivity reactions in previously sensitized persons infected with homologous and related <u>mycobacteria but they</u> cannot by themselves induce sensitization.

1.1 a. These low molecular weight materials
     b. These low molecular-weight materials
     c. These low-molecular weight materials
     d. These low-molecular-weight materials

1.2 a. mycobacteria but they
     b. mycobacteria, but they
     c. mycobacteria; but they
     d. mycobacteria: but they

2. Because health disparities exist throughout the state, the <u>TCCs</u> plan provides information to help reduce the unequal burden of cancer on priority <u>populations, which</u> include specific population groups as well as <u>geographically defined groups</u>.

2.1 a. TCCs
     b. TCC's

2.2 a. populations that
     b. populations, which

2.3 a. geographically defined groups
     b. geographically-defined groups

3. The plan incorporates <u>specific evidence based information</u> into a comprehensive approach.

     a. specific evidence-based information
     b. specific–evidence-based information
     c. specific, evidence based information
     d. specific, evidence-based information

4. Hepatitis C virus is an enormous public health problem in the United States and in our
<u>state, therefore</u> the distribution of hepatitis C infection across clients served in different
health care settings is of practical importance, guiding the allocation of screening,
counseling, and treatment resources.

    a. state, therefore
    b. state, therefore,
    c. state; therefore
    d. state; therefore,

5. <u>Franklin P. Williams, MD FACP, who</u> came from a private practice <u>in Jackson, MS, joined</u>
the dermatology staff in <u>July 2006</u>.

5.1 a. Franklin P Williams MD FACP, who
      b. Franklin P Williams, MD, FACP, who
      c. Franklin P. Williams, MD, FACP, who
      d. Franklin P. Williams, M.D., F.A.C.P., who

5.2 a. in Jackson, MS, joined
      b. in Jackson, Miss, joined
      c. In Jackson, Miss., joined
      d. in Jackson, Mississippi, joined

5.3 a. July 2006
      b. July, 2006

6. Physicians should be aware of the potential for these infections and culture rather than
treat empirically.

    a. Physicians should be aware of the potential for these infections and culture rather than
treat empirically.
    b. Physicians should be aware of the potential for these infections, and culture rather than
treat empirically.
    c. Physicians should be aware of the potential for these infections and should culture
rather than treat empirically.

7. As the human body's largest organ system, the skin protects against invasion by
<u>pathogens, helps</u> the body interpret information <u>on heat, cold, touch and pain, and</u>
prevents excessive loss of water and electrolytes.

7.1 a. pathogens, helps
      b. pathogens; helps
      c. pathogens: helps

7.2 a. on heat, cold, touch and pain
      b. on heat, cold, touch, and pain

19.   Until now, these species had survived drought, disease, and predators for millions of
       <u>years . . . and</u> to do so, most had developed powerful defense mechanisms that might have
       become future medical products.

    a. years; and
    b. years . . . and
    c. years—and

20.   The title of the article <u>is 'The median whole blood donation time</u> in the <u>best-case
       scenario</u>: findings at one blood center.'

20.1 a. is 'The
      b. is, 'The
      c. is "The
      d. is, "The

20.2 a. median whole blood–donation time
      b. median whole-blood–donation time
      c. median whole-blood–donation time
      d. median-whole-blood–donation time

20.3 a. best case scenario
      b. best-case scenario

21.   Watson and Crick worked together to describe the structure of DNA. Which of the
       following is correct?

    a. Watson and Crick's prize-winning research on the structure of DNA
    b. Watson's and Crick's prize-winning research on the structure of DNA

15.2 a. additive solutions increased
       b. additive solutions, increased
       c. additive solutions; increased
       d. additive solutions: increased

15.3 a. solution, and in particular,
       b. solution and, in particular,
       c. solution; and in particular,
       d. solution; and, in particular,

15.4 a. chloride free solutions
       b. chloride-free solutions

16.   An autosomal recessive syndrome consisting of progressive bulbar palsy with any of several cranial nerve disorders was described by three people. Which of the following correctly punctuates the name of this syndrome?

    a. Brown-Vialetto-van Laere syndrome
    b. Brown-Vialetto–van Laere syndrome
    c. Brown–Vialetto–van Laere syndrome
    d. Brown-Vialetto—van Laere syndrome

17.   The research had the following goals: identify prognostic factors; match preoperative conditions to the technique most likely to provide improvement; improve, modify, combine, or create <u>techniques which are</u> most likely to provide normal voice stability, range, and durability; and establish methods to <u>preoperatively and postoperatively</u> assess voice performance.

17.1 a. techniques that are
       b. techniques, that are
       c. techniques which are
       d. techniques, which are

17.2 a. pre- and postoperatively
       b. preoperatively and postoperatively

18.   "When we say there's a scarcity of equipment, we're not talking about MRI or CT <u>scans he explained</u>. "We're talking about stethoscopes and sphygmomanometers—basic equipment is <u>missing</u>.

18.1 a. scans" he explained
       b. scans, he explained
       c. scans," he explained
       d. scans", he explained

18.2 a. missing."
       b. missing".

11.2 a. blood, however at
      b. blood, however, at
      c. blood; however, at
      d. blood: however, at

11.3 a. complements activity
      b. complements' activity
      c. complement's activity

12.   The investigators found a <u>strong dose response relation.</u>

       a. strong dose response relation
       b. strong dose-response relation
       c. strong-dose-response relation
       d. strong, dose-response relation

13.   The patient went into remission in <u>2001, but</u> continued follow-up until signs of metastasis
       appeared in 2005.

       a. 2001 but
       b. 2001, but

14.   The lymphoid system has three principal <u>functions that include: to concentrate</u> antigens
       that enter the body into regional draining lymph <u>nodes, to circulate</u> lymphocytes or
       antigens through the lymph nodes to ensure contact between specific lymphocytes and
       appropriate <u>antigens and to carry</u> the products of the immune response, mainly antibody
       and sensitized lymphocytes, to the blood for distribution throughout the body.

14.1 a. functions; to concentrate
      b. functions: to concentrate
      c. functions that include: to concentrate
      d. functions, which include to concentrate

14.2 a. nodes, to circulate
      b. nodes; to circulate

14.3 a. antigens and to carry
      b. antigens, and to carry
      c. antigens; and to carry

15.   Proposals include the use of <u>high pH well-buffered</u> additive <u>solutions, increased</u> volumes
       of storage <u>solution, and in particular,</u> the use of <u>chloride free solutions.</u>

15.1 a. high pH well-buffered
      b. high pH, well-buffered
      c. high-pH well-buffered
      d. high-pH, well-buffered

7.3   a. pain and
       b. pain, and
       c. pain; and
       d. pain: and

8.   The etiology of this syndrome is largely <u>unknown but</u> presumably involves a complex interaction <u>among genetic</u>, metabolic, and environmental factors, including diet.

8.1   a. unknown but
       b. unknown, but

8.2   a. among genetic
       b. among: genetic

9.   To assess the impact of cardiogenic shock, all physiologic <u>variables [mean</u> arterial <u>pressure (MAP), heart</u> rate (HR), cardiac output (CO), and superior mesenteric artery <u>flow</u> <u>(SMAQ)] were</u> analyzed.

9.1   a. variables, mean
       b. variables [mean
       c. variables (mean

9.2   a. pressure, MAP, heart
       b. pressure [MAP], heart
       c. pressure (MAP), heart

9.3   a. flow (SMAQ) were
       b. flow (SMAQ)] were
       c. flow [SMAQ] were
       d. flow [SMAQ]) were

10.   Typography, graphics, layout, organization, scientific detail, and <u>content all surpass</u> the earlier edition by several orders of magnitude.

       a. content all surpass
       b. content; all surpass
       c. content: all surpass
       d. content—all surpass

11.   Simply keeping serum at room temperature <u>for 3 to 4 hours precludes</u> activation of complement in freshly drawn <u>blood; however, at</u> 4°C, the <u>complements activity</u> lasts for several days, and serum frozen soon after collection maintains full function months after storage at −70°C.

11.1   a. for 3 to 4 hours precludes
       b. for 3-to-4 hours precludes
       c. for 3-4 hours precludes